BON APPÉTIT entertaining with style

BON APPÉTIT

entertaining with style

from the Editors of Bon Appétit

Condé Nast Books/Pantheon
New York

For Condé Nast Books

Jill Cohen, President
Ellen Maria Bruzelius, Vice President
Lucille Friedman, Fulfillment Manager
Tom Downing, Direct Marketing Manager
Jennifer Metz, Direct Marketing Associate

For Bon Appétit Magazine

William J. Garry, Editor-in-Chief
Laurie Glenn Buckle, Editor, Bon Appétit Books
Marcy MacDonald, Editorial Business Manager
John Hartung, Editorial Production Director
Sybil Shimazu Neubauer, Editorial Coordinator
Marcia Lewis, Editorial Support
Nao Hauser, Text
Jennifer Rylaarsdam, Research

This book was produced and created by
Joshua Morris Publishing, Inc.,
355 Riverside Avenue, Westport, Connecticut, 06880

Designed by Salsgiver Coveney Associates

Front Jacket: Baked Spring Rolls with Chili Peanut Sauce (page 22);
Crabmeat, Corn and Cumin Salad in Endive Spears (page 27);
Caraway Corn Bread with Apricot, Bacon and Jalapeño Jam (page 26).

Page 5: Clockwise from top left: Garden Party (page 92); Family Reunion (page 64);
Dinner in the Kitchen (page 10); Back-Yard Barbecue (page 56).

All rights reserved under International and Pan-American Copyright Conventions.
Published in the United States by Pantheon Books, a division of Random House, Inc., New York,
and simultaneously in Canada by Random House of Canada Limited, Toronto.

ISBN: 0-679-44268-5

Manufactured in Italy

FIRST EDITION

2 4 6 8 9 7 5 3 1

A party begins well before the first guest is invited. It starts with the imagining of a good time: the people, the setting, the food, the talk. So this is where *Entertaining with Style* begins—not with detailed plans but with ideas for having a very good time.

Those ideas fill the first half of the book, with concepts as simple as "Dinner and a Movie," as tantalizing as a "South-of-the-Border Party" and as welcoming as a "Pasta Party." There are 12 parties in all, each sharing the same premise: The best times with friends are unpretentious and relaxed. The warmth of the people is what counts, not the elaborateness of the plans. ★ Yet no party happens without some kind of strategy. The aim of this book is to streamline that step. The menus all emphasize practicality, especially as it applies to simple, straightforward dishes that, more often than not, can be prepared ahead. You will also find tips for substituting purchased foods when time is at a premium. ★ *The Personalized Menu: Mix-and-Match Recipes* What if you like the idea of a party, but the menu doesn't quite match your schedule, your tastes or what's available in the market? We encourage you to change things around, using recipes in the second half of *Entertaining with Style.* Each of the more than 125 recipes, divided into appetizer, soup, salad and side dish, main course and dessert chapters, is accompanied by a note referring you to a party menu where it would work well. There are several substitutions for every menu item, giving you a goodly number of mix-and-match opportunities. ★ Also included in the back half of the book are four "generic" menus for the kind of parties we all have all year long: a brunch, a potluck, a cookout and a dessert buffet. The idea is that, whatever the occasion, one of these menus will fill the bill. For example, to celebrate a birthday, you might stage the brunch; to end the Little League season, you might have the team families over for the cookout; to gather everyone at your house after an evening at the theater, you might set out the dessert buffet. ★ The recipe collection in the back of the book also stands on its own as a "cookbook" of wonderful recipes ideal for entertaining. Feel free to create your own menus using dishes from each chapter and shaping them into meals that suit you and the occasion (the box on page 136 will guide you through the menu-planning process).

★ *A to Z Advice: From the Invitation to the Table* Flexibility is the essence of a casual approach to entertaining. And here, it extends to most every aspect of party-giving, from the inviting to the tablesetting. As for the invitations, whether you issue them two days ahead, two weeks or a month ahead depends on whom you're inviting— whether they travel a lot, need to find a babysitter, or would feel comfortable with a can-you-come-this-Friday phone call. And it depends on you. Do you like revving up for a last-minute round-up, or do you prefer a slow, steady count-down to party time? (Both types can learn something from the box on page 144.) ★ Tablesettings, too, can vary with your own personal approach, with the occasion, with the time of day. Don't feel bound by any rules of tradition; instead, experiment with what you have, mixing the casual with the elegant, the heirloom with the contemporary, and using things in unexpected ways. Sometimes it's the juxtaposition of things that makes them stand out and gives them real style. Throughout this book, you'll find ideas for the table, both in photographs and in helpful boxes, that you might not have thought of before. Turn to "Cocktails at

Five" for a look at how beautifully antique silver mixes with strikingly modern glass designs. And on page 122, you'll find suggestions for folding napkins that go far beyond the expected rectangle or triangle. ★ *You Choose: From Where to Eat to What to Drink* Where you stage the party is flexible, too, with options ranging from the kitchen table to a stretch of meadow in the countryside. Some people can't wait to get outdoors—and some never want to leave the living room. Much of the food here will work in either venue. The qualities that make the "Picnic in the Country" menu right for packing, for example, also make it perfect for a buffet table. Similarly, the meal that is carefree enough for "Dinner in the Kitchen" is also sturdy enough to move out to the patio. ★ There's also room for choice in accompanying beverages. While you will find suggested wines and the occasional beverage recipe in and among the menus, what you offer to drink is really a question of what you and your friends like. The "Bistro Supper" would go as well with beer (the French, after all, drink their share of beer) as it does with Bordeaux. You might also look to the drinks selection to bring another element of fun to the party, whether in the form of different after-dinner liqueurs or even a tasting of, say, beers from microbreweries, different bottlings of Beaujolais or tequilas (see page 86 for more on that topic). ★ *Have Fun: The Lighter Side of Entertaining* Don't underestimate the value of adding the element of fun to a party. If you're having fun, your guests will too, whether they're watching a Marx Brothers double feature during "Dinner and a Movie," or eating off a table covered in the Sunday comics at the "Back-Yard Barbecue." Fill your medicine cabinet with tennis balls for the first peeking guest, drop the lobsters and chase after them— just don't let your sense of humor get lost in the effort to get the meal on the table. ★ It's not very far from the memory of one good time to the imagining of another. We at *Bon Appétit* hope that the party ideas, menus, recipes and tips in *Entertaining with Style* will help get you there quickly and easily, because the best thing about a good time is that it can happen again and again.

BON APPÉTIT entertaining with style

dinner in
the kitchen

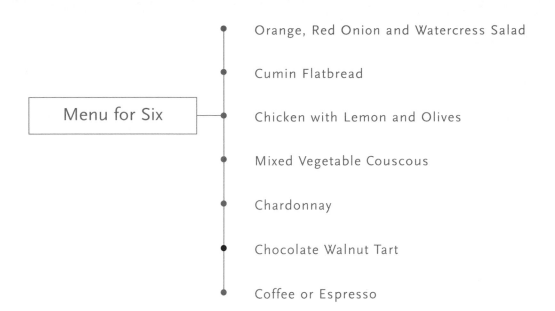

| Menu for Six |

- Orange, Red Onion and Watercress Salad
- Cumin Flatbread
- Chicken with Lemon and Olives
- Mixed Vegetable Couscous
- Chardonnay
- Chocolate Walnut Tart
- Coffee or Espresso

Come on into the kitchen—see what's cooking. ★ There is no warmer welcome than that. It's the kind of greeting you reserve for close friends, for people you know too well to let a formal dining table come between you. And this is the kind of menu that wafts an invitation from the stove to the front door. What's cooking are two richly flavored Moroccan-style dishes: juicy chicken baked with lemon and olives, and couscous with all kinds of vegetables. Everything smells so good it's hard to resist dipping a spoon into the pots for a taste. ★ Eat at the kitchen table. Or pull up stools around the kitchen island or at the counter. The colors and contours of the food decorate this meal, from the vivid salad of oranges and watercress to the chewy, tear-apart flatbread. ★ But do get out of the kitchen for dessert. Leave the dishes and settle into the living room or den with slices of dense chocolate walnut tart (below). Pour another cup of coffee and sit awhile. It's not every night you can share a good dinner with such good friends. ★ *Even Easier* If there's no time to bake, serve warm pita bread with the salad and bakery baklava or fruit and butter cookies for dessert. To add Moroccan-style fragrances to the party, brew the coffee with a few lightly crushed cardamom pods or make a pot of mint tea, using green tea and a handful of mint leaves.

Opposite: Orange, Red Onion and Watercress Salad; Chicken with Lemon and Olives

Keeping it Casual

Dinner in the kitchen is about being comfortable and relaxed. Think jeans and tennis shoes, everyday wine and flowers from the backyard. Here are some tips to help keep things low-key.

Count on entrées that can be prepared ahead of time and served family-style instead of being individually plated. A lot of last-minute cooking and plate-arranging will make the kitchen too busy for anyone to feel relaxed.

Big pieces of rustic pottery, copper baking dishes and brass trays make great serving dishes, adding casual style to the kitchen setting.

Place mats and bright napkins are as dressy as the place settings should get. To add an element of fun to the table, you can "invent" such place mats as laminated magazine photos or historic newspaper pages (great for a birthday), or pads of drawing paper with tumblers of crayons or markers.

Save the fine china and crystal for a more formal occasion, using pottery or earthenware instead (don't hesitate to bring out your favorite everyday stuff). Keep the flatware casual too—simple stainless or a pattern that incorporates another element, such as wood or horn-like handles.

Edible centerpieces are definitely appropriate in the kitchen, and can be as simple as a basket heaped with mandarin oranges or Seckel pears.

Consider the lighting from a party point of view. The overhead light you need for cooking may be too bright. If you have them, the under-cabinet lights can be supplemented with clusters of votive candles on the counter and table.

Orange, Red Onion
and Watercress Salad

A simple and refreshing way to start this Moroccan-inspired meal. The orange flower water is a flavoring extract produced from the flowers of the Seville orange. It's sold in liquor stores and in the liquor or specialty foods section of some supermarkets.

1/3	cup extra-virgin olive oil
1/4	cup orange juice
1	tablespoon red wine vinegar
1	tablespoon balsamic vinegar
1	teaspoon orange flower water (optional)
2	large bunches watercress, trimmed
4	oranges, peel and white pith removed, cut crosswise into 1/3-inch-thick rounds
1	small red onion, thinly sliced

• Whisk first 4 ingredients in bowl. Add orange flower water, if desired. Season salad dressing to taste with salt and pepper. *(Can be prepared 1 day ahead. Cover; refrigerate. Bring to room temperature before using.)*
• Arrange watercress, oranges and onion on platter. Pour vinaigrette over.
• *6 servings*

Cumin Flatbread

Thin, chewy and fragrant with spice and citrus, this bread is nice with the salad.

1 1/3 cups warm water (105°F to 115°F)
   1 envelope dry yeast
   3 tablespoons extra-virgin olive oil
   1 tablespoon minced lemon peel
      (yellow part only)
2 1/4 teaspoons coarse salt
   2 teaspoons ground cumin
   3 cups bread flour

   1 tablespoon cumin seeds
   1 tablespoon sesame seeds

• Place warm water in bowl of heavy-duty mixer. Sprinkle yeast over and stir to combine. Let stand 10 minutes. Add oil, lemon peel, salt and ground cumin. Using dough hook attachment, gradually beat in flour. Continue beating 5 minutes. Turn out dough onto lightly floured work surface and knead until smooth dough forms, about 2 minutes (dough will be very soft).
• Lightly oil large bowl. Add dough; turn to coat. Cover dough with plastic wrap and let rise in warm draft-free area until doubled in volume, about 1 hour.
• Preheat oven to 400°F. Line 12 x 18-inch baking sheet with heavy-duty foil. Brush foil with oil. Place dough in pan. Using fingertips, press out dough, covering pan completely (dough will be very thin). Sprinkle with cumin seeds and sesame seeds. Bake until golden, about 30 minutes. Loosen bread from foil. Serve bread warm or at room temperature.
• *6 servings*

Chicken with Lemon and Olives

Begin preparing this hearty, easy-to-make dish one day before serving.

1/2 cup olive oil
1/4 cup fresh lemon juice
  2 tablespoons balsamic vinegar
  1 tablespoon chopped fresh
     rosemary or 1 teaspoon dried
  1 tablespoon chopped fresh
     thyme or 1 teaspoon dried
  6 large chicken breast halves

  3 tablespoons olive oil
  1 onion, chopped
  4 garlic cloves, chopped
1/2 teaspoon turmeric
  3 cups canned low-salt
     chicken broth
  1 large lemon, thinly sliced
1/2 cup drained capers
 12 Greek green olives,* pitted
 12 brine-cured black olives
     (such as Kalamata), pitted

    Mixed Vegetable Couscous
    (see recipe on page 16)

• Whisk first 5 ingredients in bowl. Place chicken in baking dish. Season with salt and pepper. Pour marinade over; turn. Chill overnight.
• Preheat oven to 350°F. Remove chicken from marinade; pat dry. Heat 3 tablespoons oil in heavy large Dutch oven over high heat. Working in batches, add chicken, skin side down, and brown well, about 3 minutes. Using tongs, transfer chicken to bowl. Add onion and garlic to Dutch oven. Reduce heat to medium; cook until onion is tender, stirring often, about 5 minutes. Add turmeric; stir 1 minute. Add broth, lemon, capers and all olives. Bring to boil, scraping up any browned bits. Add chicken; cover. Transfer to oven; bake until cooked through, 30 minutes.
• Using tongs, place chicken in bowl. Cover to keep warm. Boil cooking liquid in Dutch oven until reduced to 2 cups, about 15 minutes. Mound couscous on platter. Top with chicken. Spoon some of cooking liquid over. Serve, passing remaining cooking liquid separately.
Available at Greek markets and some supermarkets.
• *6 servings*

Chicken with Lemon and Olives
and Mixed Vegetable Couscous

Mixed Vegetable Couscous

Couscous is a tiny, grain-shaped pasta frequently used in North African cooking. Look for it in the rice, pasta or specialty foods section of your market.

1	small butternut squash, halved lengthwise, seeded
1	small eggplant, cut into 1-inch cubes
1/4	cup olive oil
1	large turnip, peeled, cut into 1-inch pieces
1	large carrot, cut into 1-inch pieces
3	pattypan squash, quartered
3	large zucchini, cut into 1-inch pieces
3 1/4	cups plus 2 tablespoons canned low-salt chicken broth
1/4	cup (1/2 stick) unsalted butter
1/2	teaspoon turmeric
2 1/4	cups couscous (about 14 ounces)
1	15-ounce can garbanzo beans (chickpeas), rinsed, drained
1/4	cup chopped fresh Italian parsley

• Preheat oven to 350°F. Line baking sheet with foil. Place butternut squash cut side down on foil. Toss eggplant with oil in large bowl. Spread out eggplant on another baking sheet. Bake squash until tender, about 40 minutes. Bake eggplant until brown, turning occasionally, about 1 hour. Cool squash; peel. Cut squash into 1-inch pieces. Combine squash and eggplant in large bowl.
• Steam turnip and carrot until tender, about 12 minutes. Transfer to bowl with squash and eggplant. Steam pattypan squash and zucchini until tender, about 8 minutes. Transfer to bowl with vegetables. *(Vegetables can be prepared 4 hours ahead. Cover and let stand at room temperature. Rewarm on baking sheet in 350°F oven 10 minutes.)*
• Bring broth, butter and turmeric to boil in heavy large saucepan. Add couscous and stir. Cover, remove from heat and let stand 5 minutes. Transfer to bowl; fluff with fork. Add vegetables, garbanzo beans and parsley. Season with salt and pepper. Toss gently.
• *6 servings*

Chocolate Walnut Tart

Although this rich treat is not really in keeping with the evening's ethnic theme, it's still a great conclusion to the meal.

CRUST

1 1/4	cups all purpose flour
1/4	cup powdered sugar
	Pinch of salt
7	tablespoons chilled unsalted butter, cut into pieces
1	tablespoon cold water

FILLING

6	tablespoons (3/4 stick) unsalted butter
4	ounces bittersweet (not unsweetened) or semisweet chocolate, chopped
2	large eggs
1/4	cup sugar
2	tablespoons light corn syrup
1	tablespoon instant espresso powder or instant coffee powder
1/2	cup chopped toasted walnuts

Walnut halves
Powdered sugar

• FOR CRUST: Blend flour, powdered sugar and pinch of salt in processor. Add butter and cut in using on/off turns until mixture resembles coarse meal. Add 1 tablespoon cold water and blend until dough forms moist clumps. Gather dough into ball. Reserve ¼ cup dough for another use. Press remaining dough across bottom and up sides of 9-inch-diameter tart pan with removable bottom. Refrigerate 30 minutes.

• Preheat oven to 350°F. Bake crust until light golden brown, piercing with fork if bottom bubbles, about 20 minutes. Transfer to rack. *(Can be prepared 1 day ahead. Cover crust and let stand at room temperature.)*

• FOR FILLING: Preheat oven to 350°F. Stir unsalted butter and chopped chocolate in heavy medium saucepan over low heat until melted and smooth. Remove from heat. Whisk eggs, ¼ cup sugar, light corn syrup and espresso powder in medium bowl. Add chocolate mixture and chopped walnuts and stir to blend. Pour filling into crust.

• Bake tart until center of filling is set, about 20 minutes. Transfer to rack and cool. *(Can be prepared 8 hours ahead. Cover and let stand at room temperature.)* Remove tart from pan. Garnish with walnut halves. Sift powdered sugar over. Cut into wedges and serve.

• *6 servings*

Chocolate Walnut Tart

cocktails at five

Party for Ten	• Vodka and Cranberry Spritzers
	• Champagne Cocktails
	• Baked Spring Rolls with Chili Peanut Sauce
	• Grilled Chicken Skewers with Red Pepper Pesto
	• Pizza with Stilton and Caramelized Onions
	• Smoked Salmon Roulades with Watercress and Cucumber
	• Caraway Corn Bread with Apricot, Bacon and Jalapeño Jam
	• Crabmeat, Corn and Cumin Salad in Endive Spears

The cocktail hour is a time to take chances. Go ahead and invite the new guy at work or the woman you met at the health club. Bring together neighbors, colleagues and old friends. Mix up the drinks, and mix up the music, too. Beethoven, Sinatra, reggae and rock. It's the mingling that counts. ★ Cosmopolitan flavors provide more counterpoints, from crunchy spring rolls with peanut sauce and crispy little caramelized-onion pizzas (right) to crumbly bits of corn bread with jalapeño jam and creamy smoked salmon rolls. Add crab salad in endive spears (opposite) and chicken skewers with red pepper pesto and you have a wonderfully eclectic appetizer menu. Enhance the effect with a variety of serving platters, from a flat-bottomed basket to an antique silver tray, a contemporary glass plate to a hand-thrown pottery one. Use flowers similarly to multiply colors and textures in the room—and on the trays. ★ Variety may spice the party, but a single "house" cocktail can unite the guests. Be ready with a ruby-colored pitcherful of refreshing vodka-cranberry spritzers or flutes of liqueur-spiked Champagne. Offer a full bar, too, because not having someone's favorite drink may be just about the only chance you don't want to take at this untraditional cocktail party.

Cocktails For More

Because it doesn't involve a sit-down meal, a cocktail party can easily grow with your guest list. All you need do is supplement the prepared dishes with purchased items that require little more than arranging. Here are some with party appeal.

Smoked salmon: Offer the luxury of side-by-side tastings of smoked salmon from Ireland, Scotland and the Pacific Northwest, or whatever your market provides. Garnish the platter with thin lemon slices and capers, and accompany with buttered pumpernickel and rye breads.

Caviar: It needn't be top-of-the-line expensive. Golden whitefish caviar and red salmon caviar offer attractive color contrast to black varieties. For convenient serving, steam small red-skinned new potatoes in the microwave, cut them in half, and top with sour cream or crème fraîche and then spoonfuls of the caviar.

Prosciutto and other cured meats: Serve them unadorned, as they do in Italy and France. Or turn them into finger food by arranging slices on baguettes split lengthwise and lightly buttered; then cut the loaves into two-inch pieces.

Pâtés: Arrange cubes of meat pâtés on baguette slices spread lightly with mustard, and garnish with *cornichons* (those little French pickles) halved lengthwise. Seafood pâtés are good on crisp toasts with very thin radish or green onion slices. Vegetable pâtés can be served on diagonally cut cucumber slices with dill sprigs for garnish.

Crudités and fresh fruit: Such nibbles are more and more appreciated in these fat-conscious times. Set out a basket of red and yellow cherry tomatoes, a bowl of grapes (different varieties will add interest) or a platter of bell pepper rings (mix the green, red, yellow and orange peppers, if available where you shop).

Restaurant take-out: If you like the spinach pie served at a favorite Greek restaurant or the barbecued pork at a local Chinese one, place an order for a big batch (most restaurants will oblige if you give them enough time) and cut it into bite-size servings. The possibilities range from Afghan ravioli to Mexican tamales to Vietnamese shrimp toast.

Dessert: And there's always one more thing you can add, whether purchased or homemade, to give a cocktail party a sweet and graceful ending: a small dessert with coffee. The Double-dipped Strawberries on page 164 would be perfect.

Vodka and Cranberry Spritzers

1/4	cup fresh lime juice
1/4	cup sugar
1/4	cup water

3 3/4	cups cranberry juice cocktail
1 1/4	cups vodka
1/2	cup plus 2 tablespoons Campari
2 1/2	cups club soda
	Ice cubes
	Lime slices

• Combine first 3 ingredients in small saucepan. Stir over medium heat until sugar dissolves. Cool. *(Lime syrup can be made 1 week ahead. Cover and refrigerate.)*
• Mix cranberry juice, vodka, Campari and lime syrup in large pitcher. Stir in club soda. Fill glasses with ice. Pour spritzer over. Garnish with lime; serve immediately.
• *Makes 10*

Champagne Cocktails

10	sugar cubes
5	tablespoons Calvados
5	tablespoons Grand Marnier or other orange liqueur
5	cups dry Champagne or other sparkling wine, chilled
	Grated orange peel

• Place 1 sugar cube, 1½ teaspoons Calvados and 1½ teaspoons Grand Marnier in each of 10 Champagne flutes. Pour ½ cup Champagne into each. Sprinkle with grated orange peel and serve.
• *Makes 10*

Baked Spring Rolls with Chili Peanut Sauce

These crunchy treats filled with sausage and vegetables are prepared with phyllo dough instead of the traditional egg roll wrappers or wonton wrappers. The sauce is accented with distinctive Asian flavors.

2 tablespoons vegetable oil
2 tablespoons oriental sesame oil
2 cups chopped fennel
(about 1 large bulb)
1 cup chopped onion
1 small carrot, peeled, cut into matchstick-size strips
2 tablespoons minced peeled fresh ginger
2 teaspoons minced garlic
1/2 teaspoon fennel seed
1/4 pound pork sausage
1 tablespoon hoisin sauce*
1/2 teaspoon five-spice powder*

8 sheets phyllo pastry
1/2 cup (1 stick) butter, melted

Chili Peanut Sauce (see recipe at right)

• Heat vegetable oil and sesame oil in heavy large skillet over medium heat. Add fennel, onion, carrot, ginger, garlic and fennel seed; sauté until vegetables are just tender, about 10 minutes. Remove from heat. Cook sausage in heavy small skillet over medium-high heat until no longer pink, breaking up with spoon, about 8 minutes. Using slotted spoon, transfer sausage to vegetable mixture. Stir in hoisin sauce and five-spice powder. Season with salt and pepper. Cool. *(Can be made 2 days ahead. Chill.)*

• Place 1 phyllo sheet on work surface. Brush lightly with melted butter. Top with another phyllo sheet. Brush lightly with butter. Cut into 6 squares. Place 1 generous tablespoon filling across bottom of each square, leaving ½-inch border on each side. Fold sides of phyllo over filling and roll up jelly roll fashion. Place seam side down on large baking sheet. Brush spring rolls with melted butter. Repeat with remaining phyllo sheets, butter and filling. *(Can be made 1 day ahead. Cover tightly with plastic; refrigerate.)*

• Preheat oven to 400°F. Bake spring rolls until golden, about 15 minutes. Serve with Chili Peanut Sauce.

* *Available at Asian markets and also in the Asian section of many supermarkets.*

• *Makes 24*

Chili Peanut Sauce

1/2 cup roasted salted peanuts (about 2 1/2 ounces)
1/4 cup soy sauce
1/4 cup rice wine vinegar
2 tablespoons creamy peanut butter (do not use old-fashioned style or freshly ground)
2 tablespoons fresh lime juice
1 tablespoon (generous) seeded minced jalapeño chili
1 tablespoon honey
1/2 teaspoon chili powder

• Grind peanuts in processor. Add remaining ingredients and process until well blended. *(Can be prepared 2 days ahead. Cover and refrigerate. Serve at room temperature.)*

• *Makes about 1 cup*

Opposite, clockwise from top left: Pizza with Stilton and Caramelized Onions; Crabmeat, Corn and Cumin Salad in Endive Spears; Smoked Salmon Roulades with Watercress and Cucumber; Caraway Corn Bread with Apricot, Bacon and Jalapeño Jam

Grilled Chicken Skewers
with Red Pepper Pesto

This pesto is an innovative combination of ingredients that would also be nice with pasta or in a salad vinaigrette.

PESTO

1	7-ounce jar roasted red peppers, drained well
1/2	cup fresh cilantro leaves
6	tablespoons olive oil
3	tablespoons balsamic vinegar
1	small garlic clove, chopped
1/2	teaspoon dry mustard
1/2	teaspoon ground coriander
	Pinch of ground cinnamon
1/2	cup whole toasted almonds (about 2 1/2 ounces)

CHICKEN

4	skinless boneless chicken breast halves
2	tablespoons olive oil

• FOR PESTO: Puree first 8 ingredients in processor until almost smooth. Add nuts and process until finely chopped but not ground. Season with salt and pepper. *(Can be made 2 days ahead. Cover; refrigerate. Let stand 1 hour at room temperature before serving.)*

• FOR CHICKEN: Prepare barbecue (medium-high heat) or preheat broiler. Brush chicken with oil. Season with salt and pepper. Grill until cooked through, about 5 minutes per side. Cut into 1-inch pieces. Skewer each piece with toothpick. Arrange chicken on platter and serve with pesto.

• *10 servings*

Pizza with Stilton and
Caramelized Onions

To produce sweet, deep brown onions with lots of flavor, try this unique method for caramelizing them. Then pair the onions with blue cheese atop a ready-made crust.

3	tablespoons olive oil
1	garlic clove, pressed
1	tablespoon butter
1	very large onion, thinly sliced (about 2 cups)
2 1/4	cups dry white wine
1/2	cup Sherry wine vinegar
2	tablespoons sugar
1	tablespoon dry Sherry
1	12-inch-diameter baked cheese pizza crust (such as Boboli)
3	ounces Stilton cheese, crumbled
2	teaspoons chopped fresh rosemary

• Combine 2 tablespoons oil and garlic in bowl. Set aside. Melt butter with 1 tablespoon oil in heavy large skillet over medium-high heat. Add onion, ¾ cup wine, vinegar, sugar and Sherry. Boil until almost all liquid evaporates, stirring often, about 10 minutes. Add 1 cup wine, ½ cup at a time, boiling until liquid evaporates after each addition. Add ½ cup wine; cook until onions are brown and mixture is syrupy, stirring often, about 5 minutes. Season with salt and pepper. *(Garlic oil and caramelized onions can be prepared 3 days ahead. Cover separately; refrigerate.)*

• Preheat oven to 350°F. Brush crust with garlic oil. Cut into squares or diamonds, approximately 2 inches each. Arrange squares on large baking sheet. Divide onion mixture equally among squares. Top with crumbled Stilton and chopped rosemary.

• Bake until cheese begins to melt and crust is crispy, about 12 minutes. Arrange squares on platter and serve warm.

• *10 servings*

Smoked Salmon Roulades with Watercress and Cucumber

4 ounces cream cheese, room temperature
3 tablespoons sour cream
1 tablespoon fresh lemon juice
1 tablespoon sweet pickle relish
1 teaspoon Worcestershire sauce
1/4 pound thinly sliced smoked salmon

3 6-inch pita bread rounds, each cut horizontally into 2 rounds
1 large red bell pepper, seeded, cut into matchstick-size strips
1/2 cucumber, peeled, seeded, cut into matchstick-size strips
1 cup chopped trimmed watercress
6 tablespoons chopped green onions

• Blend first 5 ingredients in processor. Coarsely chop half of smoked salmon. Add to cheese mixture; process until well blended. Season with salt and pepper. Cut remaining salmon into 6 equal strips. (*Cheese mixture and salmon strips can be prepared 1 day ahead. Cover separately and chill.*)
• Spread 2 generous tablespoons cheese mixture over cut side of each pita round. Place 1 smoked salmon strip across bottom of each round. Arrange bell pepper, cucumber, watercress and green onions atop salmon, dividing equally. Roll up pita rounds tightly. Wrap in plastic; chill until firm, at least 2 hours and up to 6 hours.
• Trim ends of roulades. Cut each roulade into 1-inch-wide pieces.

• *10 servings*

Caraway Corn Bread with Apricot, Bacon and Jalapeño Jam

1 1/4 cups cornmeal
3/4 cup all purpose flour
3 tablespoons sugar
2 1/2 teaspoons baking powder
1 teaspoon caraway seeds
1 teaspoon salt
3 tablespoons chilled butter, cut into pieces
3 tablespoons bacon drippings or butter, room temperature
1 cup buttermilk
2 large eggs, separated

Apricot, Bacon and Jalapeño Jam (see recipe opposite)
Chopped fresh chives or green onions

• Preheat oven to 400°F. Place 12-inch nonstick ovenproof skillet in oven while preparing corn bread batter.
• Combine cornmeal, flour, 2 tablespoons sugar, baking powder, caraway seeds and salt in processor. Add 3 tablespoons chilled butter and cut in using on/off turns until mixture resembles coarse meal. Blend in 2 tablespoons bacon drippings or butter. Transfer mixture to large bowl. Whisk buttermilk and egg yolks in medium bowl to blend. Stir into cornmeal mixture. Beat egg whites and 1 tablespoon sugar in another bowl until stiff but not dry. Fold into cornmeal mixture in 2 additions.
• Brush skillet with 1 tablespoon bacon drippings or butter. Spoon batter into skillet. Bake until corn bread is golden and tester inserted into center comes out clean, about 10 minutes. Transfer to wire rack and cool slightly. Turn out corn bread onto work surface. Using 1¼-inch round cookie cutter, cut corn bread into rounds. (*Can be made 8 hours ahead. Cool completely. Arrange on baking sheet and cover with foil. Rewarm corn bread in 350°F oven, about 8 minutes.*)
• Top each corn bread round with dollop of jam; top with chives. Arrange on platter.
• *10 servings*

Apricot, Bacon and Jalapeño Jam

2 bacon slices, chopped

3/4 cup dried apricots (about 5 ounces), cut into thin strips
3/4 cup water
1/2 cup apricot jam
2 teaspoons minced seeded jalapeño chili

• Cook bacon in medium skillet over medium heat until brown and crisp. Drain on paper towels. Reserve 1 tablespoon drippings.
• Combine apricots and ¾ cup water in small saucepan. Boil over medium-high heat until water evaporates, about 10 minutes. Add jam and 1 tablespoon bacon drippings and stir until jam melts. Stir in bacon and jalapeño. Cool to room temperature. *(Can be made 3 days ahead. Cover; chill. Serve at room temperature.)*
• *Makes about 1¼ cups*

Crabmeat, Corn and Cumin Salad in Endive Spears

If your market stocks the rather unusual red endive, buy enough to use an equal number of the red and standard yellow endive leaves (spears), and then arrange the filled leaves alternately on colorful serving platters.

6 ounces crabmeat, picked over, well drained
1/2 cup frozen corn kernels, thawed
1/4 cup finely chopped red onion
1/4 cup mayonnaise
4 teaspoons mixed chopped fresh herbs (such as chervil, tarragon and parsley)
1 tablespoon thawed orange juice concentrate
1 tablespoon fresh lemon juice
1 teaspoon grated lemon peel
1/2 teaspoon ground cumin
1/4 teaspoon cayenne pepper

2 heads Belgian endive, separated into spears
1 tablespoon finely chopped fresh parsley
   Paprika

• Mix first 10 ingredients in medium bowl. Season with salt and pepper. Cover and refrigerate up to 1 day.
• Drain salad and place 1 rounded tablespoon in base end of each endive spear. Sprinkle with parsley and paprika. Arrange on platters and serve.
• *10 servings*

Clockwise from far left: Crabmeat, Corn and Cumin Salad in Endive Spears; Caraway Corn Bread with Apricot, Bacon and Jalapeño Jam; Smoked Salmon Roulades with Watercress and Cucumber

lunch on
the terrace

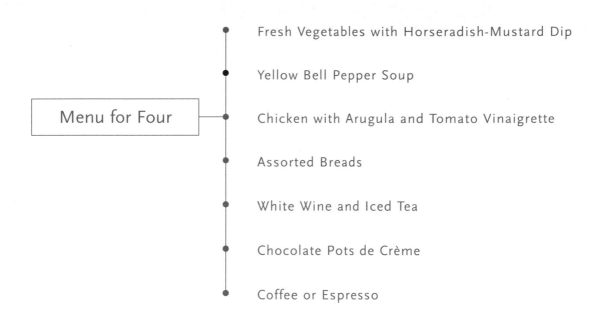

| Menu for Four |

- Fresh Vegetables with Horseradish-Mustard Dip

- Yellow Bell Pepper Soup

- Chicken with Arugula and Tomato Vinaigrette

- Assorted Breads

- White Wine and Iced Tea

- Chocolate Pots de Crème

- Coffee or Espresso

Sometimes the day itself is a cherished guest—especially in early summer, when the air is warm and still and the sun makes you want to just sit and enjoy it all. ★ It's the kind of day you've hoped for if you have planned an outdoor lunch with friends; it's also the kind of day that can inspire you to make a phone call in the morning and have your favorite neighbors over for lunch that afternoon. And whether you've planned the lunch in advance, or it's a spur-of-the-moment thing, this lovely menu will rise to the occasion. The dishes can be made ahead if you want to spend the morning in the garden; they can also be made quickly, after a trip to the store or a nearby farmers' market. ★ The tastes of this simple lunch are true to the garden-fresh mood, with nothing more complex than crudités with a tangy dip, smooth, chilled bell pepper soup (above left) and a chicken salad with tomatoes, basil and arugula that tastes like summer itself. Crusty bread and a bottle of dry white wine are the only accompaniments needed. ★ A light lunch calls out for a rich dessert—and what a decadent, creamy treat it is: chocolate *pots de crème* with raspberries and mint (or something equally sinful from the dessert chapter that doesn't require a night's refrigeration, if you're whipping things up at the last minute). Meant to be spooned slowly and appreciatively, it's the perfect pacesetter for the day. ★ *Doubling Up* If you'd like to share the day with more guests, these recipes can be doubled. But you might prefer to serve two dips instead of doubling the one, and to substitute a cake or tart that serves eight.

Fresh Vegetables with Horseradish-Mustard Dip

To make this simple appetizer even easier, pick up a mixture of pre-cut vegetables at the supermarket and use them for dipping.

- 1   8-ounce container plain nonfat yogurt
- 3   tablespoons chopped fresh chives or green onion tops
- 1   tablespoon prepared white horseradish
- 1   tablespoon Dijon mustard
- 1   tablespoon chopped fresh dill

   Assorted vegetables (such as carrot, celery, cucumber and bell pepper sticks, endive spears and cherry tomatoes)

• Mix first 5 ingredients in large bowl. Season to taste with salt and pepper. Cover and refrigerate until ready to use. *(Can be prepared 2 days ahead.)*
• Place dip in center of platter. Surround with vegetables and serve.

• *4 servings*

Yellow Bell Pepper Soup

This delicious chilled soup can be prepared a day before the party.

- 2   large yellow bell peppers (about 1 1/4 pounds total), coarsely chopped
- 2   tablespoons olive oil
- 1   onion, chopped
- 2   large garlic cloves, sliced
- 1   teaspoon dried thyme
- 1   bay leaf
- 1/3   cup dry white wine
   Generous pinch of turmeric (optional)
- 3   cups (or more) canned low-salt chicken broth

   Chopped fresh cilantro

• Cover and refrigerate ½ cup chopped bell peppers. Heat oil in heavy large skillet over medium heat. Add remaining bell peppers, onion, garlic, thyme and bay leaf and sauté until vegetables are tender, about 15 minutes. Add wine and turmeric; bring to boil. Boil 2 minutes. Add 3 cups broth, reduce heat and simmer until vegetables are very tender, stirring occasionally, about 15 minutes. Discard bay leaf. Puree soup in blender in batches. Season to taste with salt and pepper. Cover and refrigerate soup until cold. *(Can be prepared up to 1 day ahead.)*
• Thin soup with more chicken broth if too thick. Ladle into bowls. Sprinkle with reserved ½ cup bell pepper and cilantro.

• *4 servings*

Opposite, clockwise from top left: Yellow Bell Pepper Soup; Fresh Vegetables with Horseradish-Mustard Dip; Chocolate Pots de Crème

Chicken with Arugula and Tomato Vinaigrette

Pass assorted breads to go with this sophisticated chicken "salad."

 5 tablespoons olive oil
 4 6-ounce skinless boneless chicken breast halves

 2 tablespoons fresh lemon juice
 1 large garlic clove, minced
 2 large tomatoes, seeded, coarsely chopped
 2 tablespoons coarsely chopped fresh basil

 1 bunch arugula, sliced crosswise

• Heat 2 tablespoons olive oil in heavy large skillet over high heat. Season chicken with salt and pepper. Add to skillet and brown on all sides, about 2 minutes. Reduce heat to medium and cook until chicken is cooked through, turning occasionally, about 6 minutes. Transfer chicken to plate. Cover and refrigerate until cold. *(Chicken can be prepared 1 day ahead.)*
• Whisk remaining 3 tablespoons olive oil, fresh lemon juice and garlic in medium bowl. Add chopped tomatoes and basil and toss to coat. Season to taste with salt and pepper. *(Can be prepared 2 hours ahead; cover and let stand at room temperature.)*
• Slice chicken; fan slices on plates. Mix arugula into tomatoes. Spoon over chicken and serve.

• *4 servings*

Chocolate Pots de Crème

These creamy, berry-topped chocolate puddings are a snap to make.

 3 large egg yolks
 1/3 cup sugar
 Pinch of salt
 1 1/4 cups milk
 6 ounces semisweet chocolate, chopped
 1 teaspoon vanilla extract

 Fresh raspberries
 Fresh mint leaves

• Whisk egg yolks, sugar and salt in medium bowl to blend. Heat milk in heavy medium saucepan over medium heat until tiny bubbles form around edge of pan. Whisk milk into egg yolk mixture. Return mixture to saucepan and stir over medium-low heat until custard thickens and leaves path on back of spoon when finger is drawn across, about 3 minutes; do not boil. Remove from heat. Add chopped chocolate and vanilla extract and whisk until melted and smooth. Divide mixture among four ¾-cup custard cups, soufflé dishes or wineglasses. Cover desserts tightly and refrigerate overnight.
• Garnish desserts with raspberries and mint leaves and serve.

• *4 servings*

Chicken with Arugula and Tomato Vinaigrette

pasta party

Dinner for Six

- Portobello Mushrooms and Roasted Peppers with Soy-Balsamic Vinaigrette

- Garlic Bread with Oregano and Parmesan Cheese

- Rigatoni with Tomato-Meat Sauce

- Fettuccine with Garlic Shrimp and Basil-Mint Pesto

- Chardonnay and Beaujolais

- Chocolate Chip Shortbread Cookies

- Cinnamon-Vanilla Ice Cream

- Liqueurs and Brandy

Have a few friends you haven't seen in awhile and—amazingly—an evening when everyone's free? Make it a date, 35 and let pasta help make the party happen. It's undemanding of the cook and always popular, even with kids. A choice of sauces indulges guests, a salad of mushrooms and roast peppers recalls Italy, and homemade ice cream for dessert ensures a treat everyone will like. These are the details that turn everyday purchased pasta into something special. ★ What's wonderful about these recipes is that the same qualities that make them delicious also make them convenient. The flavor of the salad depends on peppers roasted ahead of time. The fettuccine with shrimp (right) features the richness of an herb pesto made days in advance. The hearty tomato-meat sauce (right) only gets better in the refrigerator overnight. And the ice cream and cookies will certainly keep—if you can keep your family away from them. ★ This child-friendly menu, with its two sauces, can easily accommodate a couple of small extra mouths. More than that, and there's always freshly cooked pasta tossed with butter and a little grated Parmesan cheese—a favorite with most children. ★ And when the kids are invited and no baby-sitter is required, it gets that much easier to come up with a mutually free night—that rare and wonderful thing.

Antipasto Add-ons

For pre-dinner nibbling, count on supermarket and deli items that need little
or no preparation. Here are some Italian-style choices to add to the roasted pepper
and mushroom platter or to replace it.

Olives: Choose from oil-cured black olives, spicy green Sicilian olives, Greek
Kalamata olives, small purplish Niçois olives and green and black Provençal olives,
mixing the varieties to add color and different tastes to the platter.

Canned caponata or deli-bought ratatouille: Either eggplant "relish" tastes
delicious cold on slices of crusty bread.

Artichokes: Perk up jarred marinated artichokes by cutting them into quarters
and tossing with a little fresh lemon juice.

Fresh mozzarella and roasted peppers: Pour the marinade from a jar of oil-packed
roasted red peppers into a bowl and stir in some chopped parsley or basil; drizzle
over sliced fresh mozzarella arranged on a plate with the roasted peppers.

Canned tuna: Buy tuna in olive oil and sprinkle it with capers and lemon juice.

Beans: Toss drained, chilled, canned garbanzo beans with black pepper and a
pinch of cayenne. Or, toss drained, chilled, canned *cannellini* (white kidney beans)
with olive oil, lemon juice and chopped parsley or basil.

Breadsticks: Italian breadsticks, called *grisini,* range from pencil-thin to finger-thick
and from a few inches to a foot long. Buy as many different ones as you can find
and arrange them in large water tumblers and low vases.

Opposite, clockwise from top left: Fettuccine
with Garlic Shrimp and Basil-Mint Pesto;
antipasto platter; cheeses and breadsticks;
Garlic Bread with Oregano and Parmesan Cheese

Portobello Mushrooms and Roasted Peppers with Soy-Balsamic Vinaigrette

The mushrooms and peppers are arranged atop greens as part of an antipasto platter. Assorted cheeses, prosciutto, salami and olives round out the selection. Serve cheese straws or breadsticks alongside.

- 1 red bell pepper
- 1 green bell pepper
- 1 yellow bell pepper

- 3 tablespoons olive oil
- 2 6- to 7-inch-diameter portobello mushrooms, stemmed, caps cut into 1/4-inch-wide slices
- 3 garlic cloves, minced
- 1 1/2 teaspoons minced fresh rosemary
- 1 1/2 teaspoons minced fresh sage

- 8 cups mixed baby greens
  Soy-Balsamic Vinaigrette (see recipe at right)

• Char peppers over gas flame or in broiler until blackened on all sides. Wrap in paper bag and let stand 10 minutes. Peel and seed peppers. Cut peppers into ¼-inch-wide strips. *(Peppers can be prepared 1 day ahead. Cover with plastic and refrigerate.)*
• Heat oil in large nonstick skillet over medium-high heat. Add mushrooms and garlic and sauté until tender, about 4 minutes. Add rosemary and sage and stir until fragrant, about 30 seconds. Remove from heat. Cool to room temperature.
• Arrange greens on large platter. Top with mushrooms and peppers. Drizzle lightly with vinaigrette and serve.
• *6 servings*

Soy-Balsamic Vinaigrette

- 3 tablespoons balsamic vinegar
- 1 tablespoon soy sauce
- 1/4 teaspoon dried crushed red pepper
- 1/3 cup olive oil

• Whisk first 3 ingredients in medium bowl to blend. Gradually whisk in oil. Season with salt and pepper. *(Can be made 1 day ahead. Cover; chill. Bring to room temperature and rewhisk before using.)*
• *Makes about ½ cup*

Garlic Bread with Oregano and Parmesan Cheese

If you are a true garlic lover, go ahead and use all eight garlic cloves.

- 3/4 cup olive oil
- 5 to 8 large garlic cloves, minced
- 2 teaspoons dried oregano
- 1 teaspoon ground pepper
- 2 1-pound French bread baguettes, split lengthwise
- 3/4 cup freshly grated Parmesan cheese

• Preheat oven to 350°F. Mix oil, garlic, oregano and pepper in small bowl. Brush cut side of bread with mixture. Sprinkle with cheese. Place loaves, cheese side up, on heavy large baking sheet. Bake until cheese melts and bread is crusty, about 15 minutes. Cut into 3-inch-long lengths.
• *6 servings*

Rigatoni with Tomato-Meat Sauce

Rigatoni with Tomato-Meat Sauce

This hearty red sauce is thick with beef, veal, onions and shallots.

1/4	cup olive oil
2	cups chopped onions
2/3	cup chopped shallots
12	garlic cloves, chopped
12	ounces ground veal
12	ounces ground beef
4 1/2	cups canned crushed tomatoes with added puree (about 1 1/3 28-ounce cans)
1 1/2	cups canned chicken broth
1 1/2	teaspoons dried oregano
1 1/2	pounds rigatoni
1	cup chopped fresh basil Freshly grated Parmesan cheese

• Heat oil in heavy large saucepan over medium-high heat. Add onions, shallots and garlic; sauté until tender and golden, about 8 minutes. Add veal and beef; sauté until cooked through, breaking up meat with back of spoon, about 5 minutes. Add crushed tomatoes, broth and oregano. Bring to boil. Reduce heat and simmer until slightly thickened, 10 minutes. Season with salt and pepper. *(Can be made 1 day ahead. Cover; chill.)*
• Cook rigatoni in large pot of boiling salted water until just tender but still firm to bite, stirring occasionally. Drain. Transfer to bowl.
• Meanwhile, bring sauce to simmer.
• Pour sauce over rigatoni. Top with basil. Serve, passing cheese separately.
• *6 servings*

Fettuccine with Garlic Shrimp and Basil-Mint Pesto

If you are making the entire dinner menu, which includes both pasta dishes, you will likely have some delicious leftovers.

4 1/2 cups (packed) fresh basil leaves
1 1/2 cups (packed) fresh mint leaves
  3/4 cup chopped walnuts, toasted
    6 tablespoons freshly grated Parmesan cheese
    3 tablespoons minced garlic
    1 cup plus 2 tablespoons olive oil

1 1/2 pounds spinach fettuccine

1 1/2 pounds uncooked large shrimp, peeled, deveined

       Fresh basil sprigs

• Finely grind 4½ cups basil, mint, nuts, Parmesan and 1½ tablespoons garlic in processor. Gradually add 1 cup oil and process until pesto is well blended. Transfer to bowl. Season with salt and pepper. *(Can be made 3 days ahead. Press plastic wrap onto surface; chill. Bring to room temperature before using.)*
• Cook fettuccine in large pot of boiling salted water until tender but still firm to bite, stirring occasionally.
• Meanwhile, heat 2 tablespoons oil in large skillet over medium-high heat. Add shrimp and 1½ tablespoons garlic; sauté until shrimp are cooked through, about 4 minutes. Remove from heat.
• Drain pasta. Return to same pot. Add pesto and toss to coat. Transfer to large bowl. Arrange shrimp over pasta. Garnish with basil sprigs and serve.
• *6 servings*

Chocolate Chip Shortbread Cookies

3/4 cup (1 1/2 sticks) unsalted butter, room temperature
1/2 cup plus 2 tablespoons sugar
1 1/2 teaspoons vanilla extract
1 3/4 cups all purpose flour
Pinch of salt
1 cup semisweet chocolate chips

• Preheat oven to 350°F. Butter two 9-inch-diameter glass pie plates. Beat butter and sugar in large bowl until fluffy. Beat in vanilla. Mix flour and salt in medium bowl. Add to butter mixture; stir just until blended. Mix in chocolate chips. Divide dough in half. Press 1 half onto bottom of each prepared pie plate. Cut each into 8 wedges, using ruler as guide and cutting through dough.
• Bake cookies until light golden, about 20 minutes. Cool completely in pie plates on racks. Recut cookies into wedges. *(Can be made 1 day ahead. Store airtight at room temperature.)*
• *Makes 16*

Cinnamon-Vanilla Ice Cream

Here's a simple flavor combination that works great. Team the ice cream with the cookies and some brandy or fruit liqueur, and it's even better.

3 cups whipping cream
1 1/2 cups whole milk
2 vanilla beans, split lengthwise
1 cup plus 2 tablespoons sugar
6 large egg yolks
2 1/2 teaspoons ground cinnamon

8 cinnamon sticks (optional)

• Combine cream and milk in heavy large saucepan. Scrape in seeds from vanilla beans; add beans. Bring just to simmer. Whisk sugar and yolks in large bowl to blend. Gradually whisk in hot cream mixture. Return mixture to same saucepan. Stir over medium-low heat until custard thickens and leaves path on back of spoon when finger is drawn across, about 6 minutes; do not boil. Strain into large bowl. Whisk in ground cinnamon. Chill until cold, about 3 hours.
• Transfer custard to ice cream maker and process according to manufacturer's instructions. Transfer ice cream to covered container and freeze until firm. *(Can be made 3 days ahead. Keep frozen.)*
• Scoop ice cream into bowls. Garnish with cinnamon sticks, if desired.
• *Makes about 5 cups*

Cinnamon-Vanilla Ice Cream
and Chocolate Chip Shortbread Cookies

bistro supper

●	Tomato, Cheese and Herb Tart
●	White Burgundy
Menu for Eight ─ ●	Beef Tenderloin Steaks with Peppercorn Sauce
●	Herbed Potato Galette
●	Mixed Greens with Champagne Vinaigrette
●	Assorted Cheeses, Bread, Fruit and Nuts
●	Red Bordeaux
●	Cassis Sorbet with Cookies
●	Coffee and After-Dinner Drinks

This romantic menu is the culinary equivalent of armchair travel. Its classically French dishes will instantly

transport you—and company—to that friendly little bistro you found in Paris... or hope to find someday.

★ A bistro is where the neighborhood dines, where the talk flows with the wine, and where the

regulars ask, "What's good tonight?" ★ At your house, everything is good tonight, beginning

with a tart of tomatoes and cheese (left). Then there are rosy-rare steaks with a brandy-

peppercorn sauce and crispy potatoes. A salad follows, as is the custom in France, then a sorbet

made with crème de cassis, that delicious black currant-flavored liqueur. ★ There's no restaurant staff in the

kitchen, of course, so these recipes allow for a lot of advance work: The tart crust, the sauce for the steaks, the

salad dressing and the sorbet can all be made ahead. Even the potatoes can be completed up to the final browning

an hour or two beforehand. Round out the menu with such store-bought French staples as breads, cheeses and

cookies—possibly almond *tuiles* or *langues-de-chat*—to accompany the sorbet. ★ A good red wine from Bordeaux

would lend another note of authenticity to the meal. Enjoy it with the steaks, and then finish it, as is customary,

with a selection of cheeses (see the box on page 47 for suggestions). Because wine and cheese are always a fine

French excuse for sitting around the table long into the night.

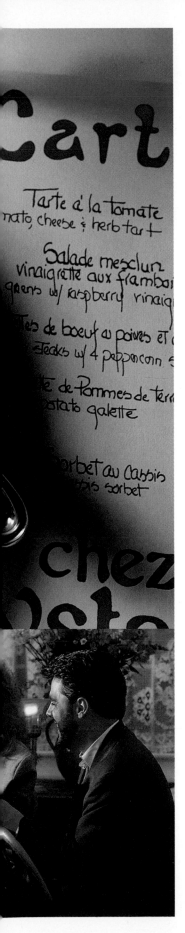

Tomato, Cheese and Herb Tart

CRUST

1 1/4 cups all purpose flour

1/4 teaspoon salt

1/2 cup (1 stick) chilled unsalted butter, cut into pieces

4 tablespoons (about) ice water

FILLING

5 medium tomatoes, cut into 1/2-inch-thick slices

9 ounces Emmenthal or Gruyère cheese, thinly sliced

1 tablespoon minced fresh basil or 1 teaspoon dried

1 teaspoon minced fresh thyme or 1/4 teaspoon dried

1 teaspoon minced fresh oregano or 1/4 teaspoon dried

3 tablespoons freshly grated Parmesan cheese

• FOR CRUST: Combine flour and salt in processor. Add butter and cut in using on/off turns until mixture resembles coarse meal. Add enough water by tablespoons to form moist clumps. Gather dough into ball; flatten into disk. Wrap in plastic and refrigerate 30 minutes.

• Preheat oven to 375°F. Roll out dough on lightly floured surface to 13-inch round. Transfer to 11-inch-diameter tart pan with removable bottom. Trim crust edges. Freeze crust for 15 minutes.

• Line crust with foil. Fill with dried beans or pie weights. Bake until crust is set, about 15 minutes. Remove foil and beans and bake until pale golden, about 15 minutes more. Cool crust on rack. *(Can be prepared 1 day ahead. Cover and let stand at room temperature.)*

• FOR FILLING: Cut each tomato slice in half. Place tomato slices on paper towels and let drain for 45 minutes.

• Preheat oven to 375°F. Top crust with Emmenthal cheese slices. Arrange tomatoes atop cheese, overlapping slightly. Sprinkle herbs, then Parmesan cheese over tomatoes.

Season with pepper. Bake until cheese melts and tomatoes are tender, about 35 minutes. Cool slightly. Remove tart pan sides. Cut tart into wedges and serve.

• *8 servings*

Beef Tenderloin Steaks with Peppercorn Sauce

2 tablespoons (1/4 stick) unsalted butter

1/4 cup chopped shallots

1/3 cup brandy

1 cup canned unsalted beef broth

1 cup crème fraîche or whipping cream

1 tablespoon (or more) four-peppercorn blend* or whole black peppercorns, crushed

8 6-ounce beef tenderloin steaks

1/4 cup vegetable oil

• Melt butter in heavy medium saucepan over medium heat. Add shallots and sauté until golden, about 8 minutes. Add brandy and bring to boil. Add broth and boil until mixture is reduced to 1 cup, about 5 minutes. Add crème fraîche or cream and 1 tablespoon peppercorns; cook over medium heat until reduced to sauce consistency, about 3 minutes if using crème fraîche or 8 minutes if using cream. Taste, adding more peppercorns if desired. Season with salt. *(Can be made 1 day ahead. Cover and refrigeate.)*

• Prepare barbecue (medium-high heat) or preheat broiler. Brush steaks with oil. Season with salt and pepper. Grill to desired doneness, about 4 minutes per side for medium-rare. Bring sauce to simmer. Transfer steaks to plates. Spoon some sauce over. Serve, passing remaining sauce separately.

* *A blend of black, white, pink and green peppercorns. Available in the spice section of many supermarkets.*

• *8 servings*

Opposite, clockwise from top left: Beef Tenderloin Steaks with Peppercorn Sauce and Herbed Potato Galette; Cassis Sorbet

Herbed Potato Galette

4	tablespoons (1/2 stick) unsalted butter
4	tablespoons safflower oil
1/2	cup finely chopped onion
3	pounds russet potatoes, peeled, cut into 1/8-inch-thick slices
4	large garlic cloves, minced
2	teaspoons minced fresh rosemary or 1 teaspoon dried
1	teaspoon salt
1/4	cup finely chopped parsley

• Divide butter and oil between two 9-inch-diameter nonstick skillets and cook over medium heat until butter melts. Divide onion between skillets and sauté until tender, about 5 minutes. Increase heat to medium-high. Divide potatoes, garlic, rosemary and salt between skillets and cook until potatoes are light golden, turning often, about 10 minutes. Using metal spatula, press and flatten potatoes into uniform thickness. Cover; reduce heat to medium and cook until potatoes brown on bottom, 15 minutes.
• Place 1 large plate over 1 skillet. Using oven mitts, hold plate and skillet together and turn skillet over, releasing potato galette onto plate. Slide galette back into skillet. Repeat with remaining potato galette. Cook until potatoes brown on bottom, pressing with spatula, about 15 minutes. Slide galettes out onto plates. Sprinkle with parsley.
• *8 servings*

Mixed Greens with Champagne Vinaigrette

1/3	cup Champagne vinegar or white wine vinegar
3	tablespoons minced shallots
3	tablespoons minced fresh chives or green onion tops
1	teaspoon dried pink peppercorns, coarsely chopped
1	cup canola oil
12	cups assorted mixed greens (such as curly endive, butter lettuce, red leaf lettuce, radicchio and arugula)

• Whisk first 4 ingredients in small bowl. Gradually whisk in canola oil. Season dressing to taste with salt.
• Place greens in large bowl. Toss with enough dressing to season to taste.
• *8 servings*

Cassis Sorbet

Simple sugar cookies are nice with this.

1 1/2	16-ounce packages frozen unsweetened boysenberries or blackberries, thawed
1 1/2	cups sugar
3/4	cup water
5	tablespoons crème de cassis
	Additional crème de cassis (optional)
	Fresh mint sprigs (optional)

• Puree thawed berries in blender or processor. Strain through fine sieve set over bowl, pressing firmly on solids with back of spoon. Combine sugar and water in heavy medium saucepan. Stir over medium heat until sugar dissolves. Stir sugar syrup and 5 tablespoons cassis into berry puree. Chill berry mixture.
• Transfer berry mixture to ice cream maker and process according to manufacturer's instructions. Freeze in covered container.
• Scoop sorbet into bowls. Drizzle with more cassis and garnish with mint sprigs.
• *8 servings*

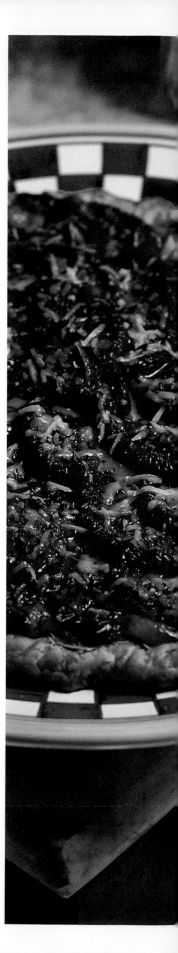

Tomato, Cheese and Herb Tart

The Cheese Course

An opulent French cheese platter will offer diners three or four contrasting tastes and textures, but it's fine to serve just one perfect cheese, such as a creamy Brie. All the cheeses don't have to be French—even in France the selection may be international, with the emphasis on quality rather than place of origin.

Serve the cheese at room temperature. Set places with small plates and knives and forks. Fill the bread basket with sliced baguette and, if desired, slices of crusty whole grain, nut and raisin loaves. Tart apples, pears and grapes all go well with cheese because they have a wine-like balance of sweetness and acidity. The crunch of walnuts, hazelnuts and almonds is also apt, as is a glass of Port or hard cider.

To sample a spectrum of cheeses, choose at least one from each of the following categories.

Soft, creamy types: Brie and Camembert are the most common, but also try Saint Nectaire, Chaource and Reblochon from France, as well as Taleggio from Italy. You might also consider the buttery richness of a French triple cream, such as Saint André.

Firm types: These include the world's many variations on Swiss and cheddar, such as Appenzell and Emmenthal from Switzerland, English Cheshire and Leicester, French Cantal and aged Dutch Gouda.

Blue cheeses: Select from among French Roquefort and Bleu de Bresse, Italian Gorgonzola, English Stilton and American Maytag.

Goat and sheep-milk cheeses: The tanginess of these cheeses adds another dimension of taste to the platter. Choices range from crumbly, aged chèvre from France to fresh American goat cheese with herbs to firm, sharp sheep-milk cheese from Spain.

48

picnic
in the
country

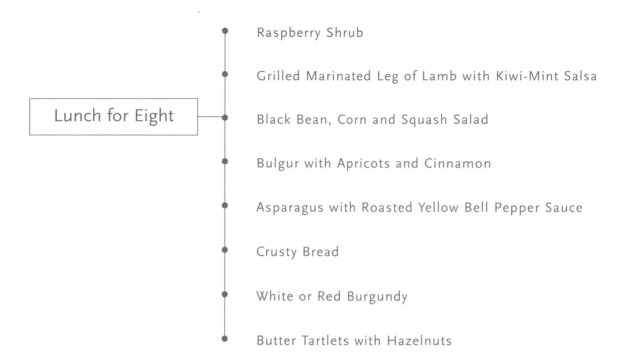

- Raspberry Shrub

- Grilled Marinated Leg of Lamb with Kiwi-Mint Salsa

Lunch for Eight

- Black Bean, Corn and Squash Salad

- Bulgur with Apricots and Cinnamon

- Asparagus with Roasted Yellow Bell Pepper Sauce

- Crusty Bread

- White or Red Burgundy

- Butter Tartlets with Hazelnuts

Country is a state of mind. It can come to you at a rustic summer cabin or at a local park concert under the sky, at a beachside picnic spot or a meadow off a mountain road. But it always involves a getaway from indoor routines. That's what makes it "country." ★ Pack up dinner and you're halfway there, no matter where you spread out the food. So this menu is designed for travel. It will keep in a cooler while you find the right spot, and it needs no fussy arranging. Yet its tastes are lavish. Grilled lamb with a lovely green salsa of kiwi and mint, a confetti salad of black beans and corn, chilled asparagus with yellow pepper sauce, a bulgur salad with apricots and pistachios—these are dishes worthy of china and silver, but they will entice just the same on paper plates. Round out the meal with a refreshing raspberry cooler and hazelnut tartlets for dessert, and you have a movable feast fit for a birthday, an anniversary—or any other fine day. ★ *Pitching In* A picnic's shared spirit of adventure makes it perfectly O.K. to ask guests to help tote blankets, tableware, charcoal and beverages to the site. Don't hesitate to go a step further and divide up several recipes, too, since none of them is difficult to make, and several cooks can only shorten the amount of time it takes you to get to the country.

49

Packing A Picnic

Before you take off, make a list of everything you don't want to get caught without in some bucolic setting. Don't forget a corkscrew, bottle opener, barbecue utensils and mitts, slicing knives, serving spoons, trash bags, paper towels, foil for wrapping leftovers and, of course, the insect repellent. Once you've got these items packed, turn to the food. Here are some tips for easy transport.

Keep meat, salads, soda, wine and other beverages in coolers packed with blue ice; fill thermos jugs with the syrup and ice cubes for the Raspberry Shrub. Pack dessert and breads in a picnic basket or box cushioned with a tablecloth; use wadded newspaper or zipper-top plastic bags with air in them to hold things securely. Wrap breakable dishes and glassware in cloth napkins, towels, tablecloths, blankets and other fabric items you're planning to bring anyway.

Look into attractive, unbreakable tableware, including plastic dishes, metal tumblers, tin plates, wooden bowls for serving salads and baskets for baked goods. You can enhance plastic containers by nestling them in napkin-lined baskets.

Feel free to mix china and glassware with paper and plastic. You may find the right balance of elegance and practicality in, say, real plates and flatware with plastic cups and paper napkins.

If you're planning to cook at the picnic site, be sure to bring, along with the charcoal, either solid charcoal starter or a chimney starter and some newspaper.

Opposite, clockwise from top left: Butter Tartlets with Hazelnuts; Black Bean, Corn and Squash Salad, Bulgur with Apricots and Cinnamon with slices of Grilled Marinated Leg of Lamb with Kiwi-Mint Salsa; Asparagus with Roasted Yellow Bell Pepper Sauce; Raspberry Shrub

Raspberry Shrub

Popular in eighteenth-century England, a shrub is a fruit drink traditionally made with citrus juice, rum and sugar. This modern version is nonalcoholic. To prepare the sweet raspberry vinegar that is its base, you need to start at least two days ahead. Use leftover vinegar to accent a salad dressing when a slightly sweet flavor is desired.

6	cups fresh raspberries (about 4 baskets) or frozen unsweetened, thawed
1 3/4	cups distilled white vinegar
2 1/2	cups sugar
	Ice cubes
24	fresh mint leaves
6	cups chilled club soda

• Place half of berries in large glass bowl. Pour 1¼ cups vinegar over. Cover and let stand 24 hours at room temperature.
• Strain mixture through coarse sieve set over bowl, pressing on solids with back of spoon to release as much pulp as possible. Add remaining berries and ½ cup vinegar. Cover; let stand 24 hours at room temperature.
• Strain mixture through coarse sieve set over heavy large saucepan, pressing on solids. Add sugar; stir over medium-high heat until sugar dissolves. Boil until reduced to 2¾ cups, about 10 minutes. Pour vinegar into bottle; cool. Seal bottle. (*Can be made 1 month ahead. Store in dark place at cool room temperature.*)
• Fill 8 glasses with ice. Add 3 mint leaves, 3 tablespoons raspberry vinegar and ¾ cup club soda to each glass.
• *8 servings*

Grilled Marinated Leg of Lamb with Kiwi-Mint Salsa; Black Bean, Corn and Squash Salad; Asparagus with Roasted Yellow Bell Pepper Sauce; Bulgur with Apricots and Cinnamon

Grilled Marinated Leg of Lamb with Kiwi-Mint Salsa

Ask your butcher to butterfly the lamb.

1/4	cup olive oil
1/4	cup chopped fresh rosemary or 1 tablespoon dried
1/4	cup chopped fresh mint
4	garlic cloves, minced
2	teaspoons ground pepper
1 1/2	cups dry red wine
1/2	cup red wine vinegar
1	5-pound leg of lamb, boned, butterflied

Kiwi-Mint Salsa (see recipe below)

• Process first 5 ingredients in processor until well blended. Add wine and vinegar and blend well. Place lamb, skin side down, in glass baking dish. Pour marinade over. Cover; chill at least 4 hours and up to 8 hours, turning occasionally.
• Prepare barbecue (medium-high heat). Grill lamb to desired doneness, about 13 minutes per side for medium-rare. Place lamb on platter. Let stand 10 minutes. (*Can be prepared 2 hours ahead. Cover and let stand at room temperature.*) Slice lamb. Serve with salsa.
• *8 servings*

Kiwi-Mint Salsa

9	kiwis, peeled, cut into 1/2-inch pieces
3	tablespoons finely chopped fresh mint leaves
2	tablespoons honey
1 1/2	teaspoons chopped fresh rosemary

• Mix all ingredients in bowl. (*Can be made 4 hours ahead. Cover and chill.*)
• *Makes about 3 cups*

Black Bean, Corn and Squash Salad

1 1/2   cups dried black beans, rinsed, picked over

3   ears corn, husked
1   cup chopped red onion
1   large red bell pepper, chopped
1/2   cup plus 2 tablespoons chopped Italian parsley
1/4   cup white wine vinegar
1   tablespoon fresh lemon juice
1/2   cup plus 1 tablespoon olive oil

1   pound whole baby summer squash or baby zucchini, or 4 large zucchini, cut into 1/2-inch-thick rounds
3   garlic cloves, chopped

• Place beans in heavy large saucepan; add enough cold water to cover by 3 inches. Soak beans overnight.

• Drain beans and return to pan. Add enough cold water to cover beans by 3 inches and bring to boil. Reduce heat to medium; simmer until beans are tender, stirring occasionally, about 1½ hours. Drain well. Transfer to large bowl; cool.

• Cook corn in pot of boiling water until crisp-tender, about 5 minutes. Drain and cool. Cut corn kernels off cobs. Add corn, onion, bell pepper and ½ cup parsley to beans. Whisk vinegar and lemon juice in small bowl. Gradually whisk in ½ cup oil. Pour dressing over salad and toss well. Season with salt and pepper. *(Can be prepared 1 day ahead. Cover and refrigerate. Bring salad to room temperature before continuing.)*

• Heat 1 tablespoon oil in heavy large skillet over medium heat. Add squash and garlic and sauté 3 minutes. Reduce heat to medium-low. Cover and cook until squash is crisp-tender, about 8 minutes. Season squash with salt and pepper. Sprinkle with remaining 2 tablespoons parsley. Spoon squash atop salad. Serve at room temperature.

• *8 servings*

Bulgur with Apricots and Cinnamon

1   tablespoon butter
1/2   cup finely chopped shallots
2   garlic cloves, minced
2   cups bulgur (cracked wheat)
1   6-ounce package dried apricots, sliced
1   teaspoon salt
1/4   teaspoon ground cinnamon
2 1/2   cups water

2/3   cup fresh orange juice
2   tablespoons olive oil
1/2   cup coarsely chopped pistachios (about 2 ounces)
1/2   cup chopped fresh Italian parsley

• Melt butter in heavy medium saucepan over medium-high heat. Add shallots and garlic and sauté until tender, about 3 minutes. Mix in bulgur, apricots, salt and cinnamon. Add 2½ cups water and bring to boil. Reduce heat to low, cover and cook until all water is absorbed and bulgur is tender, stirring frequently to prevent sticking, about 20 minutes. Transfer bulgur to bowl and cool.

• Mix orange juice and oil into bulgur. *(Can be made 1 day ahead. Cover and chill.)* Mix pistachios and parsley into bulgur. Season with salt and pepper.

• *8 servings*

Black Bean, Corn and Squash Salad

Asparagus with Roasted Yellow Bell Pepper Sauce

2 large yellow bell peppers
1/4 cup plus 1 tablespoon olive oil
1 tablespoon fresh lemon juice

2 pounds asparagus, trimmed

• Char peppers over gas flame or in broiler until blackened on all sides. Wrap in paper bag and let stand 10 minutes. Peel, seed and chop peppers. Place peppers and ¼ cup oil in blender and puree until smooth. Add lemon juice and blend until smooth. Season with salt and pepper.
• Cook asparagus in large pot of boiling water until crisp-tender, about 4 minutes. Drain. Transfer to bowl of ice water; cool. Drain. *(Sauce and asparagus can be made 6 hours ahead. Cover and let stand at room temperature.)*
• Toss asparagus with remaining 1 tablespoon oil. Season with salt and pepper. Arrange asparagus on platter. Spoon some of sauce over. Serve, passing remaining sauce separately.
• *8 servings*

Butter Tartlets with Hazelnuts

Nonstick vegetable oil spray
1 cup packed golden brown sugar
1/3 cup pure maple syrup
3 tablespoons unsalted butter, room temperature
1 teaspoon all purpose flour
2 large eggs
1/2 cup hazelnuts (about 2 ounces), toasted, chopped

1 1/2 15-ounce packages refrigerated pie crusts (3 crusts)

Lightly sweetened whipped cream (optional)
Fresh blueberries or currants (optional)

• Preheat oven to 450°F. Spray sixteen ⅓-cup muffin cups with nonstick vegetable oil spray. Beat sugar, syrup, butter and flour in medium bowl to blend. Add eggs 1 at a time, beating well after each addition. Mix in nuts. Set filling aside.
• Let pie crusts stand at room temperature for 15 minutes. Unfold crusts on lightly floured work surface and press on seams to flatten. Using cookie cutter or glass, cut out sixteen 3¼-inch rounds from pie crusts. Fit pie crust rounds into prepared muffin cups, pressing onto bottom and partially up sides.
• Spoon 2 tablespoons filling into each cup. Bake until filling browns and crust forms on top, about 12 minutes. Cool completely in pans on racks. Run small sharp knife around muffin cups to loosen tartlets. Turn tartlets out, then turn right side up. *(Can be made 1 day ahead. Store airtight at room temperature.)*
• Serve tartlets with whipped cream and fresh berries, if desired.
• *Makes 16*

back-yard
barbecue

Menu for Six	Fresh Berry Freeze
	Grilled Oysters and Clams with Lime Butter
	Grilled Sausages
	Grilled Salmon Steaks with Cumin Mayonnaise
	Sugar Snap Pea, Corn and Tomato Salsa
	Red Potato Salad with Dill
	Mixed Green Salad with Blue Cheese Vinaigrette
	White Wine, Beer and Iced Tea
	Star-spangled Shortcakes
	Chilled Champagne Sabayon with Berries

When the mouthwatering smells coming from the grill announce briny clams and oysters and rich salmon steaks—well, there isn't much more a cook has to do.

★ That's the beauty of this menu: It is based on foods that taste so good hot off the fire that the embellishments can be kept simple and minimal. Lime butter for the shellfish and a crisp, summery salsa with the salmon add just enough to enhance without overwhelming the main attractions. A creamy red potato salad and a quick tossing of greens are enough to make a satisfying warm-weather meal, with assorted breads and a chilled Sauvignon Blanc. ★ But Champagne would not be out of place here. In fact, there's a hint of the bubbly in the sabayon, a dessert that's a breeze to make but classy enough for a toast with additional Champagne. Pass a plate of star-shaped shortbread cookies (above) and settle back to celebrate a long evening of lazing around while the actual stars come out.

★ *A Shellfish Note* Oysters and clams are best purchased the same day you plan to cook them. If they are not available, grill skewers of shrimp or ears of corn instead, basting and serving them with the lime butter.

Grilling Tips

To make the grilling as easy as the meal, try these tricks of the trade.

Line a charcoal grill with heavy-duty aluminum foil, being careful not to cover vents, before adding charcoal. Cleanup will be simplified and the food will cook a little faster.

Build the fire to one side of a charcoal grill, or leave part of a gas grill turned off, so that food that has browned can be moved away from the fire to a cooler part of the grid. Cover the grill and the food will finish cooking more evenly in the indirect heat.

For smoky flavor, soak a handful of wood chips in water for an hour and toss over the fire just before adding the food. (For gas grills, follow manu-facturer's directions.) Alder and mesquite are nice with salmon.

Spray the cooking grid—off the fire—with vegetable oil spray to prevent sticking. If you are grilling meats that have not been marinated, pat them dry and spray with vegetable oil spray to promote browning.

Tilt the grid slightly, by propping it up on one side or at the back, so that cooking juices flow to the side or front and not into the fire, where they can cause flare-ups.

Opposite, clockwise from top left:
Grilled Salmon Steaks with Cumin Mayonnaise
and Sugar Snap Pea, Corn and Tomato Salsa;
Mixed Green Salad with Blue Cheese Vinaigrette;
Red Potato Salad with Dill; Fresh Berry Freeze;
Grilled Oysters and Clams with Lime Butter

Fresh Berry Freeze

2   1/2-pint baskets fresh raspberries
2   cups raspberry juice or
     other berry juice
3   tablespoons (or more) honey
10 ice cubes
4   orange slices

• Puree raspberries, juice and 3 tablespoons honey in blender. Add more honey, if desired. Add ice cubes; puree until frothy. Pour into glasses. Garnish with orange slices; serve immediately.

• *6 servings*

Grilled Oysters and Clams with Lime Butter

1   cup (2 sticks) butter
2   tablespoons fresh lime juice
2   tablespoons grated lime peel

18 fresh oysters in shells, scrubbed
18 fresh clams in shells, scrubbed

• Melt butter in heavy small saucepan over low heat. Whisk in lime juice and lime peel. Season with salt and pepper. *(Can be prepared 1 day ahead. Cover and refrigerate. Before using, melt over low heat, whisking constantly.)*
• Prepare barbecue (medium-high heat). Place shellfish on barbecue and grill until shells open, turning occasionally, about 5 minutes (discard any that do not open). Transfer oysters and clams to platter. Drizzle with lime butter.

• *6 servings*

Grilled Salmon Steaks with Cumin Mayonnaise

Grilled sausages can accompany the salmon, if you like.

1/2 cup plus 1 tablespoon
      mayonnaise
1 1/2 teaspoons ground cumin
1 1/2 teaspoons dried oregano
6   8-ounce salmon steaks (about
      3/4 inch thick)
      Sugar Snap Pea, Corn and Tomato
      Salsa (see recipe below)

• Prepare barbecue (medium-high heat). Combine mayonnaise, cumin and oregano in bowl. Season with salt and pepper. Spread mixture on both sides of salmon. Grill salmon until just cooked through, about 4 minutes per side. Serve salmon with salsa.

• *6 servings*

Sugar Snap Pea, Corn and Tomato Salsa

3   ears corn, husked
30 sugar snap peas, cut crosswise
     into 1/2-inch pieces
2   large tomatoes, seeded, diced
1   small red onion, halved, thinly sliced
1   red bell pepper, cut into 1 1/2-inch-
     long matchstick-size strips

1/3 cup olive oil
1/4 cup red wine vinegar
1/4 cup fresh lime juice
1/4 cup chopped fresh oregano
1   tablespoon minced garlic
1   tablespoon ground cumin
1   teaspoon chili powder
1/4 teaspoon hot pepper sauce
     (such as Tabasco)

Opposite: Sugar Snap Pea, Corn and Tomato Salsa (top); Grilled Sausages and Grilled Salmon Steaks with Cumin Mayonnaise (bottom)

• Cook corn in large pot of boiling salted water until crisp-tender, about 3 minutes. Combine corn kernels, sugar snap peas, tomatoes, onion and red bell pepper in large bowl. *(Vegetables can be prepared 8 hours ahead. Cover and refrigerate.)*

• Whisk oil, vinegar, lime juice, oregano, garlic, cumin, chili powder and hot pepper sauce in medium bowl to blend. Drain any liquid from vegetables. Add dressing to vegetables; toss to coat. Season with salt and pepper. Let stand at room temperature 1 hour before serving.

• *6 servings*

Red Potato Salad with Dill

For another salad, toss mixed greens with a blue cheese vinaigrette.

2	pounds red-skinned potatoes, cut into bite-size pieces
1	red bell pepper, chopped
1	onion, chopped
6	tablespoons mayonnaise
6	tablespoons plain yogurt
1/4	cup chopped fresh dill
1	tablespoon Dijon mustard
1	tablespoon balsamic vinegar
1	tablespoon prepared white horseradish

• Cook potatoes in large pot of boiling salted water until tender, about 10 minutes. Drain; cool slightly. Combine potatoes, bell pepper and onion in large bowl. Whisk mayonnaise and all remaining ingredients in medium bowl. Pour half of dressing over warm potato mixture; toss to coat. Let stand 1 hour. *(Can be made 1 day ahead. Cover salad and remaining dressing separately; chill. Bring to room temperature before continuing.)*

• Toss salad with remaining dressing.

• *6 servings*

Star-spangled Shortcakes

If you don't have a star-shaped cookie cutter,
most any four-inch one will work.

2 1/4	cups unbleached all purpose flour
1/2	cup sugar
1 1/2	teaspoons baking powder
1	teaspoon ground cinnamon
3/4	teaspoon baking soda
1/2	teaspoon salt
6	tablespoons (3/4 stick) chilled unsalted butter, cut into pieces
2/3	cup chilled buttermilk
1	large egg yolk
1/2	teaspoon vanilla extract
1/8	teaspoon almond extract
3	tablespoons whipping cream
1/3	cup sliced almonds

• Preheat oven to 425°F. Line baking sheet
with parchment. Mix first 6 ingredients in
processor. Using on/off turns, cut in
butter until mixture resembles coarse meal.
Whisk buttermilk, yolk, and vanilla and
almond extracts in bowl. With machine
running, add to flour mixture; process until
moist clumps form.
• Place dough on floured surface; gather into
ball. Using floured hands, press out to
¾-inch thickness. Using floured 3½- to
4-inch-diameter star-shaped cookie cutter,
cut out stars. Gather scraps and press out to
¾-inch thickness; cut out more stars.
• Transfer stars to prepared sheet. Brush with
cream. Top with almonds. Bake until light
golden, about 12 minutes. Cool on rack. *(Can be
made 1 day ahead; wrap and store at room temperature.)*
• *Makes about 8*

Chilled Champagne Sabayon with Berries

The terms used on Champagne labels to indicate sweetness can be confusing at best, misleading at worst. Dry, or *doux*, Champagne is, in fact, sweet. "Brut" indicates a very dry bottle of the bubbly. (You want the former for this recipe.)

  6 large egg yolks
10 tablespoons sugar
  6 tablespoons dry Champagne
  1 cup chilled whipping cream

  2 1/2-pint baskets raspberries
  2 1/2-pint baskets blueberries
     Star-spangled Shortcakes
     (see recipe on page 62)

• Using electric mixer, beat yolks and sugar in large metal bowl. Set bowl over saucepan of simmering water (do not allow bottom of bowl to touch water). Whisk until thick and thermometer registers 160°F, about 8 minutes. Remove from over water. Gradually whisk in Champagne. Place bowl in larger bowl filled with ice; let stand until cool, stirring occasionally, about 15 minutes. Beat cream in medium bowl to medium peaks. Fold into egg mixture in 2 additions. *(Can be made 4 hours ahead. Cover; chill.)*

• Divide berries among bowls. Spoon sabayon over. Serve with shortcakes.

• *6 servings*

Chilled Champagne Sabayon with Berries and Star-spangled Shortcakes

family reunion

- Fresh Crab Dip

- Chardonnay

- Fish and Clam Stew

- Skillet Shrimp and Oysters

- Low-Country Red Rice

- Sweet Onion Tart with Herb Crust

- Sautéed Mixed Vegetables

- Merlot

- Blueberry Slump

Dinner for Ten

Lots of hugs, the same old jokes, catching up with everyone—that's what it means to come home. The memories are important, and so is the food. There should be plenty—enough to elicit protests (as in, "I can't eat another bite!"). And since what gets served will become part of the family's shared history, it should be a little memorable itself.

★ This menu, with its bold and varied tastes of South Carolina's low-country cooking, will be remembered for years to come. Someone will no doubt have to have the recipe for the couldn't-be-simpler crab dip—and bring it out at every party from here on in. Another will remember the sweet onion tart with its rich custard topping as "the best thing you ever made." The seafood stew (right), dense with clams and potatoes, will make it into the family archives for post-football game suppers as well as reunions. The formula for the sizzling skilletful of shrimp, oysters and sausage will also get tucked away, because it delivers satisfaction in a hurry. Even the rice is a contender for family classic, with its unusual accents of bacon and hot sauce. ★ By all rights, those who complain about having eaten too much shouldn't get dessert. But of course there's no chance of that when any family gathers. So a big pan of old-fashioned berry slump (opposite), oozing juices beneath its biscuit topping, will be just another memory not long after it gets scooped out and passed around.

Fresh Crab Dip

3/4 cup low-fat mayonnaise or
     regular mayonnnaise
  3 tablespoons prepared horseradish
  3 tablespoons finely chopped onion
  1 tablespoon Worcestershire sauce
12 ounces crabmeat
    Hot pepper sauce (such as Tabasco)

    Assorted crudités (such as Belgian
    endive spears, celery sticks, carrot
    sticks and bell pepper strips)
    Assorted crackers and breadsticks

• Mix first 4 ingredients in medium bowl.
Mix in crab. Season to taste with hot pepper
sauce, salt and pepper. *(Can be prepared 1 day
ahead. Cover and refrigerate.)*
• Place dip in center of platter. Surround
with crudités, crackers and breadsticks.
• *10 servings*

Fish and Clam Stew

A great-looking and great-tasting
first-course dish.

  2 tablespoons olive oil
  2 green bell peppers, chopped
  2 large carrots, peeled, thinly sliced
  1 cup chopped onion
  1 cup chopped celery
  2 14 1/2-ounce cans ready-
    cut tomatoes
  2 cups bottled clam juice
  1 cup dry white wine
  3 medium russet potatoes,
    peeled, diced
  4 garlic cloves, minced
  1 teaspoon dried oregano
  1 bay leaf
1/2 teaspoon cayenne pepper

24 small clams, scrubbed
  2 pounds firm white fish fillets
    (such as red snapper or grouper),
    cut into 1-inch pieces
    Chopped fresh parsley

• Heat oil in heavy large pot over medium-high
heat. Add peppers, carrots, onion and celery
and cook until vegetables are tender, stirring
frequently, about 15 minutes. Mix in tomatoes,
clam juice and wine. Add potatoes, garlic,
oregano, bay leaf and cayenne and bring to
boil. Reduce heat and simmer until potatoes are
tender, about 20 minutes. *(Can be made 1 day
ahead. Cover and chill. Bring to simmer before continuing.)*
• Add clams to soup, cover and cook until
clams open, about 5 minutes (discard any that
do not open). Add fish. Cover; cook until fish
is cooked through, about 3 minutes. Sprinkle
with parsley and serve.
• *10 servings*

*Opposite, clockwise from top left: Fish and Clam
Stew; Low-Country Red Rice, Sweet Onion Tart
with Herb Crust and Skillet Shrimp and Oysters
with Sautéed Mixed Vegetables*

Skillet Shrimp and Oysters

Sautéed mixed vegetables make an attractive and easy side dish

1/4	cup olive oil
1/2	cup chopped shallots
8	large garlic cloves, minced
2	pounds uncooked large shrimp, peeled, deveined
2	dozen oysters, shucked
1	pound smoked kielbasa sausage, sliced
1	cup dry white wine
6	tablespoons chopped fresh parsley
2	tablespoons chopped fresh oregano or 2 teaspoons dried
1	tablespoon chopped fresh rosemary or 1 teaspoon dried Lemon wedges

• Heat olive oil in heavy large skillet over medium heat. Add shallots and garlic and sauté 3 minutes. Add shrimp and oysters and sauté until shrimp turn pink, about 3 minutes. Using slotted spoon, transfer shrimp and oysters to bowl. Add kielbasa sausage and white wine to skillet and boil until liquid is reduced to ¼ cup, about 8 minutes. Return shrimp and oysters to skillet. Mix in parsley, oregano and rosemary and cook until shrimp and oysters are heated through, about 2 minutes. Transfer to platter. Garnish with lemon wedges and serve.

• *10 servings*

Low-Country Red Rice

14	bacon slices
2	large red bell peppers, chopped
1	medium onion, chopped
4	teaspoons dried thyme
3/4	cup tomato paste
3	cups long-grain white rice
6	cups canned vegetable broth or chicken broth
1	tablespoon hot pepper sauce (such as Tabasco)

• Cook bacon in heavy large Dutch oven over medium-high heat until brown. Transfer bacon to paper towels and drain. Crumble

bacon. Pour off all but 3 tablespoons drippings from Dutch oven. Add bell peppers, onion and thyme and sauté 5 minutes. Mix in tomato paste, then rice. Add broth, hot pepper sauce and bacon and bring to boil. Reduce heat, cover and simmer until rice is tender, about 30 minutes. Season with salt.

• *10 servings*

Sweet Onion Tart with Herb Crust

CRUST

2 2/3	cups all purpose flour
1	teaspoon minced garlic
1/2	teaspoon salt
1/2	cup (1 stick) chilled unsalted butter, cut into pieces
1/2	cup chilled solid vegetable shortening, cut into pieces
6	tablespoons mixed chopped fresh herbs (such as basil and chives)
6	tablespoons (about) ice water

FILLING

1/4	cup (1/2 stick) unsalted butter
1 3/4	pounds Vidalia onions or other sweet onions, thinly sliced
1	cup water
1	cup half and half
1	cup whipping cream
4	large eggs
4	large egg yolks
1/2	teaspoon salt
1/2	teaspoon pepper
1/8	teaspoon ground nutmeg
1/2	cup freshly grated Parmesan cheese (about 1 1/2 ounces)

• FOR CRUST: Blend flour, garlic and salt in processor. Add butter and shortening and cut in using on/off turns until mixture resembles coarse meal. Mix in herbs. Gradually blend in enough water until dough forms moist clumps. Gather dough into ball. Divide in half. Flatten into disks. Refrigerate for 30 minutes.

- Preheat oven to 375°F. Roll out each dough disk on lightly floured surface to 12-inch round. Transfer to 9-inch-diameter tart pans with removable bottoms; trim edges. Place crusts in freezer for 15 minutes.
- Line crusts with aluminum foil. Fill with dried beans or pie weights. Bake until sides are set, about 15 minutes. Remove foil and beans and continue baking until golden, piercing any bubbles in crusts with fork, about 10 minutes. Cool completely.
- FOR FILLING: Preheat oven to 350°F. Melt butter in heavy large skillet over medium-high heat. Add onions and 1 cup water. Cover and cook until onions are tender, stirring occasionally, about 15 minutes. Uncover and cook until almost no liquid remains in skillet, stirring frequently, about 10 minutes.
- Whisk half and half, cream, eggs, yolks, salt, pepper and nutmeg in large bowl. Divide onion mixture between 2 tart shells. Ladle egg mixture over. Sprinkle with cheese. Bake until tops begin to brown, about 30 minutes. Transfer to racks and cool until just warm.
- *Makes two 9-inch tarts*

Blueberry Slump

Blueberry Slump

A slump is a dessert of cooked, sweetened fruit topped with biscuit dough or pastry, then simmered on top of the stove or, sometimes, baked. This dish gets its name from the way the baked dough topping "slumps" into the fruit filling.

FILLING
3   12-ounce packages frozen unsweetened blueberries, thawed
1   cup plus 8 tablespoons sugar
1/2   cup water
3   tablespoons cornstarch dissolved in 3 tablespoons water

12   ounces cream cheese, room temperature
1 1/2   tablespoons fresh lemon juice
1 1/2   teaspoons vanilla extract

TOPPING
1 1/2   cups all purpose flour
1/3   cup firmly packed brown sugar
1   tablespoon baking powder
1/4   teaspoon (generous) salt
3/4   cup milk
3   tablespoons unsalted butter, melted

- FOR FILLING: Bring blueberries, 1 cup plus 2 tablespoons sugar and ½ cup water to boil in heavy large saucepan, stirring frequently. Add cornstarch and bring to boil, stirring frequently. Pour mixture into 13 x 9 x 2-inch glass baking dish and cool. *(Can be made 4 hours ahead. Cover; keep at room temperature.)*
- Preheat oven to 400°F. Using electric mixer, beat cream cheese, lemon juice, vanilla and 6 tablespoons sugar in medium bowl until well blended. Drop mixture by small spoonfuls over berry mixture, spacing evenly.
- FOR TOPPING: Mix first 4 ingredients in large bowl. Stir in milk and butter. Drop mixture by spoonfuls atop filling, spacing evenly. Bake until filling bubbles and topping is golden, about 25 minutes. Cool slightly.
- *10 servings*

pizza party

Dinner for Six

- Roma Salsa with Garlic Toasts
- Color Wheel Crudités
- Soave
- Pizza Picasso
- Mixed Greens and Fennel Salad
- Chianti
- Vanilla Jackson Pollock
- Fresh Fruit
- Espresso with Sambuca

If there is such a thing as a fun food, it would have to be pizza. And when you add a buffet of do-it-yourself toppings to the

basic pizza idea, it's an instant party—and an easy one. ★ The only rule is that there are no rules. With sauces and toppings

arrayed on a side table or kitchen counter, everyone becomes a designer with artistic license to build

their own Boboli (one of those ready-made, baked cheese pizza crusts) however they like. Maybe

a stripe of each sauce: red pepper-tomato, green pesto, and black olive-anchovy. Dots of

pepperoni, flecks of cheese, bold strokes of prosciutto or onion: It's pizza as you see—and want

to taste—it. For dessert, the canvas changes to squares of vanilla ice cream, but creative effort is

still what counts, as guests drizzle on their own combinations of raspberry, lemon and chocolate

sauces. ★ Since this is an ideal after-work party, you might want to give everyone a chance to unwind before the fun begins.

Offer drinks and set out a bowl of tomato-basil salsa with crisp garlic toasts. A make-ahead platter of crudités, arranged in a

color wheel pattern, provides something to crunch on beforehand, with leftovers making more terrific pizza toppings later.

★ As fun as this party is, the cleverest part of its design is the ease of it all. The basics—pizza crusts and ice cream—are

purchased. The sauces can be made days ahead, leaving little more to do than toss a salad before the pizza-making begins.

Supermarket Shortcuts

To further streamline preparations for this party, substitute a choice of purchased sauces (check the refrigerator section of your market for tomato sauces and fresh pesto) for the ones here. Also, consider the following supermarket-ready toppings, either instead of or in addition to the ones in the pizza recipe (page 75).

Cooked small or medium shrimp: Delicious with pesto sauce.

Barbecued chicken: Find this at the deli or meat counter; it's good with tomato sauce and chopped onions.

Broccoli florets: Pick these up from the salad bar, then steam them in the microwave just until bright green. Drizzle with olive oil.

Frozen leaf spinach: Thaw, and then squeeze out as much liquid as possible. Drizzle with oil and stir in chopped garlic; it's terrific with feta cheese and olives.

Arugula: Easier to chop than parsley, it makes a great seasoning to sprinkle over a pizza topped with chicken, cheese or seafood.

Canned anchovies and chopped olives: These pizza "naturals" could substitute for the olive-anchovy sauce.

Deli salads and spreads: Vegetables in vinaigrette, ratatouille, *tapenade* (that Provençal puree of olives, anchovies and capers)and artichoke puree are sold in many supermarket delis, and all complement oil-brushed pizza crusts. Eggplant and Mediterranean-style bean dips work well on pizzas topped with spicy sausage and olives.

Opposite, clockwise from top left:
Color Wheel Crudités;
Vanilla Jackson Pollock;
Roma Salsa with Garlic Toasts;
two takes on Pizza Picasso

Roma Salsa with Garlic Toasts

GARLIC BUTTER
- 2 large garlic cloves
- 1 large shallot
- 1/2 cup (1 stick) unsalted butter, room temperature

SALSA
- 1/2 large red onion, cut into 4 pieces
- 1/2 cup lightly packed fresh basil
- 1 pound ripe plum tomatoes, halved, seeded
- 3 tablespoons freshly grated Parmesan cheese
- 3 tablespoons fresh lime juice
- 2 tablespoons olive oil
- 1 tablespoon balsamic vinegar

- 16 1/2-inch-thick French bread baguette slices

• FOR GARLIC BUTTER: Finely chop garlic and shallot in processor. Add butter and blend until smooth. Season with salt and pepper. *(Can be prepared 1 day ahead. Cover and refrigerate. Bring to room temperature.)*
• FOR SALSA: Coarsely chop onion and basil in processor. Add tomatoes; chop coarsely using on/off turns. Transfer salsa to bowl. Mix in cheese, lime juice, oil and vinegar. Season with salt and pepper. *(Can be made 2 hours ahead. Cover and chill. Drain before serving.)*
• Preheat broiler. Arrange bread slices on baking sheet. Spread with garlic butter. Broil until brown and crisp. Arrange garlic toasts and salsa on platter.
• *6 servings*

Color Wheel Crudités

Snack on the crudités before dinner. The leftovers are used as pizza toppings.

- Pitted olives
- 12 carrots, peeled, cut into sticks
- 12 celery stalks, cut into sticks
- 6 yellow summer squash, sliced
- 8 ounces mushrooms, thinly sliced
- 3 Japanese eggplants, thinly sliced
- 2 red bell peppers, cut into strips
- 2 green bell peppers, cut into strips
- 1 red onion, cut into thin rings

• Place olives in bowl and set in center of platter. Form "color wheel" by arranging vegetables around olives, grouping together all pieces of each vegetable.
• *6 servings*

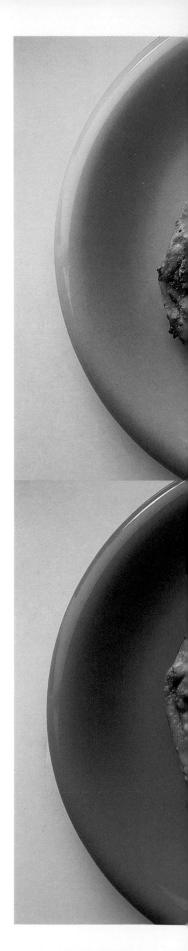

Pizza Picasso, with Olive-Anchovy Sauce, yellow squash, tomatoes, pepperoni and cheese (top), and Pesto Sauce, mushrooms, yellow squash, cheese and basil (bottom)

Pizza Picasso

This was named after the artist because guests are presented with a variety of sauces and toppings that they can use to design their own abstract-looking pizzas.

    Red Bell Pepper and Tomato Sauce (see recipe below)
    Pesto Sauce (see recipe on page 76)
    Olive-Anchovy Sauce (see recipe on page 76)
8   ounces smoked chicken, diced
8   ounces pepperoni, thinly sliced
8   ounces mozzarella cheese, shredded
8   ounces provolone cheese, shredded
3   ounces Parmesan cheese, grated
3   ounces Romano cheese, grated
4   ounces prosciutto slices, chopped
6   medium-size Boboli (baked cheese pizza crusts)
    Color Wheel Crudités (see recipe on page 74)

• Preheat oven to 425°F. Place first 10 ingredients in separate bowls on counter. Set out Boboli crusts and crudités and allow guests to assemble their own pizzas, using sauces and toppings of their choice. Place pizzas on baking sheets. Bake until cheeses melt and crusts are crisp, about 20 minutes.

• *6 servings*

Red Bell Pepper and Tomato Sauce

1   8-ounce can tomato sauce
1   7-ounce jar roasted red bell peppers, drained
2   tablespoons fresh oregano leaves or 2 teaspoons dried
2   tablespoons dry red wine
1/8 teaspoon cayenne pepper
2   tablespoons olive oil

• Puree first 5 ingredients in processor. Mix in oil. Season with salt and pepper. *(Can be made 2 days ahead. Cover and refrigerate.)*

• *Makes about 1¾ cups*

Pesto Sauce

> 4 cups lightly packed fresh basil leaves
> 1/2 cup toasted pine nuts
> 6 garlic cloves
> 1/2 cup olive oil
> 1 tablespoon unsalted butter, room temperature
> 1/2 cup freshly grated Parmesan cheese
> 1/4 cup freshly grated Romano cheese
> 1 teaspoon fresh lemon juice
> 1/8 teaspoon white pepper

• Finely grind basil, nuts and garlic in processor. Gradually blend in oil, then butter. Add both cheeses, lemon juice and pepper and blend well. Season with salt. *(Can be prepared 1 week ahead. Place in container. Top with a thin layer of olive oil to seal; cover and refrigerate.)*
• *Makes about 1 ⅓ cups*

Olive-Anchovy Sauce

> 1 1/2 cups brine-cured black olives (such as Kalamata), pitted
> 6 tablespoons olive oil
> 4 anchovy fillets
> 1 1/2 tablespoons fresh lemon juice

• Blend all ingredients to coarse puree in processor. Season to taste with pepper. *(Can be prepared 2 days ahead. Cover and refrigerate. Stir sauce well before using.)*
• *Makes about 1 ¼ cups*

Mixed Greens and Fennel Salad

> 1 small fennel bulb, trimmed, finely chopped
> 2/3 cup minced red onion
> 1/2 cup olive oil
> 1/4 cup balsamic vinegar
> 2 tablespoons white wine vinegar
> 2 garlic cloves, minced
>
> 1 small head romaine lettuce, torn into bite-size pieces
> 2 heads radicchio, torn into bite-size pieces
> 2 arugula bunches, torn into bite-size pieces

• Mix first 6 ingredients in bowl. Season with salt and pepper. Cover and let stand at least 30 minutes and up to 2 hours.
• Combine lettuce, radicchio and arugula in large bowl. Toss with enough dressing to season to taste and serve.
• *6 servings*

Vanilla Jackson Pollock

For this clever dessert, guests squeeze assorted sauces from plastic bottles to create their own ice cream "canvases" in the manner of abstract expressionist Jackson Pollock. Purchase ice cream in either a half-gallon rectangular carton or a round tub. Remove the carton and slice the ice cream into rectangles or rounds.

> 1 1/2-gallon carton or tub vanilla ice cream
> Raspberry Sauce (see recipe on page 77)
> Lemon Sauce (see recipe on page 77)
> Purchased chocolate syrup

• Remove ice cream from carton. Cut ice cream into 1-inch-thick slices and arrange on chilled plates. Serve, passing sauces separately.
• *6 servings*

Raspberry Sauce

1   12-ounce package frozen
    unsweetened raspberries, thawed
1/4   cup plus 2 tablespoons
      orange juice
1/3   cup sugar
2   tablespoons cornstarch
2   tablespoons seedless
    raspberry jam

• Puree raspberries with ¼ cup orange juice in processor or blender. Strain raspberry mixture through sieve into heavy medium saucepan, pressing on solids with back of spoon. Mix in sugar. Combine cornstarch and remaining 2 tablespoons orange juice in small bowl; mix until smooth. Add to raspberry mixture and bring to boil, stirring. Mix in seedless raspberry jam. Cover and refrigerate sauce until well chilled. *(Raspberry sauce can be prepared 2 days ahead. Keep covered and refrigerated.)*
• *Makes about 1½ cups*

Lemon Sauce

1   11 1/4-ounce jar lemon curd
2   tablespoons frozen lemonade
    concentrate, thawed

• Combine lemon curd and thawed lemonade concentrate in small bowl. Whisk lemon sauce until smooth.
• *Makes about 1 cup*

After-Work Entertaining

It *is* possible, having a few friends over for dinner after a long day on the job. It just requires a little planning and a measure of organization. Here are some tips on how you can make it happen with style and ease.

Be realistic. Don't try to do too much. These kinds of get-togethers are meant to be casual and relaxed, so make sure the food and the setting—and you—are, too. Know your own pace in the kitchen, and plan the menu around what you can easily accomplish in the couple of hours you have between getting home and getting dinner on the table.

Choose a main course that can be made beforehand and reheated, or one that's easy to do at the last minute. The pizzas here, which combine purchased products and do-ahead sauces, are one good example; others would be a soup, a stew, chili or pasta with a make-ahead sauce or a "dressed-up" purchased one. Another option is to grill or broil pork, or lamb chops, chicken breasts or fish and top with a simple, salsa-like sauce.

Serve a mixed green salad—they're easy to prepare, everyone likes salads and they go with just about anything. Wash the greens and make the vinaigrette the night before; refrigerate separately.

For dessert, don't hesitate to buy something at a bakery or grocery store and embellish it. Purchased sorbet can be made special with fruit and cookies. Top pound cake with whipped cream and berries. Or simply pass a platter of fresh fruit, nuts and chocolates.

Set the table the night before the party. The next morning, before you leave for work, get the coffee maker ready to go so that all you have to do is flip the switch after dinner. Then, on the way home, pick up some flowers.

dinner
and a
movie

Menu for Six	• Martinis
	• Crackers and Cheese
	• Stuffed Mushrooms with Bacon and Olives
	• Caesar Salad with Sourdough Croutons
	• Scampi with Red Bell Peppers and Zucchini
	• Lemon Rice Pilaf
	• Sour Cream Cheesecake
	• Coffee

The lights are low, the room is hushed and all eyes are on the TV screen—until a voice calls out, "This cheesecake is fantastic!" Then, murmurs of agreement drown out the movie hero just as he is about to....

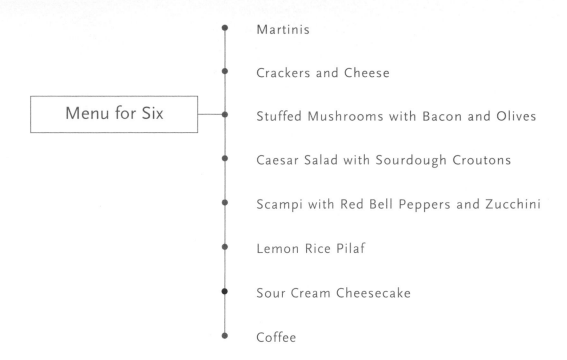

Oh well, you can always rewind and play it again. That's part of the fun of a video party: There are two scenarios and two casts of characters, one onscreen and one off. The evening's entertainment is a double feature of both. ★ Fit for Bogart, Hepburn, Chaplin or Hitchcock, the menu includes three other popular classics: stuffed mushrooms, Caesar salad and that action-stopping cheesecake (right). But, unlike great movies, the dishes get even better in updated remakes. Olives and bacon jazz up the mushrooms; the salad is a lighter and spicier take on the original; and walnuts and orange peel grant the cheesecake hints of glamour. The main course is as breezy as the banter in a Cary Grant film—a simple one-dish sauté of shrimp, red pepper and zucchini that gets served with a lemony rice pilaf. ★ This meal is a winning reel to unwind on a Friday night, because there isn't much last-minute kitchen suspense. The food has been cast for its do-ahead flexibility and simplicity. Add cheese and crackers, maybe a pitcher of Martinis. Light some candles, then settle in for a lively argument with good friends about what, exactly, you should watch.

Stuffed Mushrooms with Bacon and Olives

A classic appetizer updated and made easy with one-day do-ahead instructions. You could also add cheese and crackers.

18	large mushrooms (each about 2 inches in diameter)
4	bacon slices
1	tablespoon chopped garlic
1	teaspoon chopped fresh rosemary or 1/2 teaspoon dried
1/4	cup chopped pitted brine-cured black olives (such as Kalamata)
2	ounces cream cheese, room temperature

Olive oil

• Remove stems from mushrooms. Coarsely chop stems and set aside. Cook bacon in heavy large skillet over medium heat until crisp. Using tongs, transfer bacon to paper towels and drain. Pour off all but 1 tablespoon drippings from skillet. Add chopped mushroom stems, garlic and rosemary and sauté over medium heat until tender, about 10 minutes. Crumble bacon and add to skillet. Add olives and stir to combine. Mix cream cheese in medium bowl until smooth. Add mushroom mixture and stir to blend. Season to taste with salt and pepper.
• Lightly brush rounded side of mushroom caps with oil. Place rounded side down on large baking sheet. Spoon filling into caps, mounding in center. *(Can be prepared 1 day ahead. Cover stuffed mushrooms with plastic and chill.)*
• Preheat oven to 375°F. Bake stuffed mushrooms until heated through, about 20 minutes. Transfer to platter and serve.
• *Makes 18*

Opposite, clockwise from top left: Martinis; Caesar Salad with Sourdough Croutons; Scampi with Red Bell Peppers and Zucchini and Lemon Rice Pilaf; Stuffed Mushrooms with Bacon and Olives; Sour Cream Cheesecake

Caesar Salad with Sourdough Croutons

1/2	cup fresh lemon juice
2	tablespoons Worcestershire sauce
4	garlic cloves, coarsely chopped
1/2	teaspoon hot pepper sauce (such as Tabasco)
1	cup olive oil
2	large heads romaine lettuce, torn into bite-size pieces
1	red onion, thinly sliced Sourdough Croutons (see recipe below)
1	cup freshly grated Parmesan cheese (about 3 ounces)

• Blend first 4 ingredients in processor or blender. With machine running, gradually add oil in thin steady stream. Season to taste with salt and pepper. *(Can be prepared 1 day ahead. Cover and chill. Bring to room temperature before using.)*
• Combine lettuce, onion and croutons in large bowl. Toss with enough dressing to season to taste. Sprinkle with cheese and serve.
• *6 servings*

Sourdough Croutons

6	cups 3/4-inch cubes sourdough bread (about 6 ounces)
2	tablespoons olive oil
6	tablespoons freshly grated Parmesan cheese (about 1 1/2 ounces)
1/2	teaspoon garlic powder

• Preheat oven to 350°F. Place bread cubes in large bowl. Drizzle olive oil over; toss to distribute. Add grated Parmesan cheese and garlic powder and toss to coat. Spread out cubes on heavy large baking sheet. Bake until golden brown, using metal spatula to turn bread cubes occasionally, about 15 minutes. Cool completely. *(Can be prepared 1 day ahead. Store in airtight container at room temperature.)*
• *Makes about 6 cups*

Scampi with Red Bell Peppers and Zucchini

Since this shrimp dish can be prepared ahead and then baked just before serving, it's ideal for a buffet.

3/4	cup (1 1/2 sticks) butter
2	red bell peppers, cut into 2-inch-long, 1/2-inch-wide strips
3/4	pound zucchini, cut into 1/2-inch rounds
3/4	cup chopped shallots (about 4)
1/4	cup finely chopped garlic
1/4	cup drained capers
2	pounds large uncooked shrimp, peeled, deveined, tails left intact
1/3	cup chopped fresh basil

• Melt butter in heavy large skillet over high heat. Add bell peppers, zucchini, shallots and garlic; sauté until shallots begin to soften, about 4 minutes. Mix in capers. Transfer mixture to large baking dish or gratin dish. *(Can be made 4 hours ahead. Cool completely. Cover; set aside.)*

• Preheat oven to 450°F. Mix shrimp into vegetables. Bake until shrimp are cooked through, stirring occasionally, about 10 minutes. Sprinkle with basil.

• *6 servings*

Lemon Rice Pilaf

5	tablespoons olive oil
1 1/2	cups minced onion
3	cups long-grain white rice
3	14 1/2-ounce cans chicken broth
1/2	cup fresh lemon juice
1 1/2	tablespoons grated lemon peel
3/4	teaspoon ground pepper

• Heat oil in heavy large saucepan over medium heat. Add onion and sauté until tender, about 10 minutes. Add rice and sauté 2 minutes. Add remaining ingredients and bring to boil, stirring occasionally. Reduce heat to low, cover and cook until rice is tender and liquid is absorbed, about 20 minutes. Remove from heat and let stand covered 5 minutes. Season to taste with salt.

• *6 servings*

Sour Cream Cheesecake

This smooth, creamy cheesecake is a big, old-fashioned crowd pleaser. Make it a day before the party, because it needs to chill in the refrigerator overnight. For a pretty decoration, garnish the cheesecake with orange slices and mint sprigs.

CRUST
2	cups graham cracker crumbs
1/2	cup walnuts (about 2 ounces)
1/4	cup packed golden brown sugar
2	teaspoons ground cinnamon
7	tablespoons butter, melted

FILLING
3	8-ounce packages cream cheese, room temperature
1	cup sugar
	Pinch of salt
1	16-ounce container sour cream
2	teaspoons grated orange peel
1	teaspoon vanilla extract
3	large eggs

• FOR CRUST: Preheat oven to 350°F. Wrap outside of 9-inch-diameter springform pan with 2¾-inch-high sides with foil. Finely grind cracker crumbs, nuts, sugar and cinnamon in processor. Add butter and process until moist crumbs form. Press crust onto bottom and 2¼ inches up sides of pan. Bake crust until beginning to brown, about 15 minutes. Cool. Maintain oven temperature.

• FOR FILLING: Blend cream cheese, sugar and salt in processor until smooth, stopping occasionally to scrape down sides. Add sour cream, orange peel and vanilla; process until well blended. Add eggs; blend until combined. Pour into crust. Bake until center no longer moves when pan is shaken and edges puff slightly, about 1 hour 5 minutes. Transfer to rack. Gently cut around pan sides to loosen crust. Place hot cheesecake directly in refrigerator; chill overnight.

• Release pan sides from cake. Transfer cheesecake to platter and then serve.

• *12 servings*

Scampi with Red Bell Peppers and Zucchini

84

south-
of-the-
border
party

Dinner for Six

- Picadillo
- Pico de Gallo
- Cheese Enchiladas with Green Sauce
- "Drunken" Beans
- Fiesta Chicken Salad with Lime-Cilantro Vinaigrette
- Beer and Margaritas
- Mexican Chocolate Cake

When what you have is a Saturday night and a group of friends coming for dinner, what you need is something to make the evening a little different. That's where a menu like this one comes in, with its appealing Tex-Mex tastes: chilies, cumin, tortillas, beans, tomatoes and cheese. ★ This is the kind of food that disappears fast. Pour the Margaritas, set out a spicy *picadillo* of ground beef with a fresh chili-sparked salsa—and be ready with lots of chips (right). Then bring on cheese-filled enchiladas with a creamy green sauce, a pot of beer-simmered beans and a salad that's a treasury of southwestern ingredients—chicken, avocado, corn, pumpkin seeds, cilantro and crumbled cheese. For dessert, offer squares of luscious yet easy-to-make chocolate cake (opposite) with cups of rich, dark coffee. ★ "Easy" applies across the board here, both in terms of preparation and practicality. There isn't a complex recipe in the batch, and all of them can, at least in part, be prepared ahead; in fact, the intrigue of seasonings only ripens when you do so. Also, the quantities are generous. So you can easily expand the fiesta to serve 10 or 12 by doubling the enchilada and salad recipes and adding a purchased salsa, rice and a platter of tropical fruits, such as papaya and pineapple, as well as plenty of Mexican beer.

The Tequila Tasting

Maybe only tequila itself could rival the popularity of Margaritas, which are tequila with lime juice and triple sec or Cointreau. And that's exactly what's been happening of late. People are discovering the subtlety and smoothness of premium tequila, either straight-up or on the rocks. Premium tequilas are made from juice pressed from the agave plant, without the sugar syrup added to cheaper tequilas. The best of them are bottled in Mexico.

A tequila tasting can be fun—and interesting. To organize a tasting, choose one or more brands from the dozens available in each of these categories.

Blanco: This is fresh, unaged tequila, crisp and dry in taste. It is not heresy to serve it with a twist of lime or in luxurious Margaritas.

Reposado: Aged in oak barrels at least two months, tequila reposado is smoother and potentially more flavorful than blanco.

Añejo: After spending at least a year in oak, tequila añejo may become as dark and complex as Cognac or the finest whiskey. It deserves to be sipped slowly from snifters—and no Margaritas, please.

Picadillo

This spicy ground beef appetizer is hearty and satisfying.

- 2 tablespoons olive oil
- 1 pound lean ground beef
- 1 onion, chopped
- 1 red or yellow bell pepper, chopped
- 6 large garlic cloves, minced
- 1 16-ounce can diced peeled tomatoes
- 3/4 cup raisins
- 1 4-ounce jar chopped pimientos, drained
- 1/4 cup tomato paste
- 2 jalapeño chilies, seeded, minced
- 2 tablespoons sugar
- 1 tablespoon dried oregano
- 1 tablespoon ground cumin
- 1 tablespoon ground coriander
- 1/2 teaspoon ground cinnamon
- 1/2 teaspoon ground cloves

- 3/4 cup slivered almonds, toasted
  Tortilla chips

• Heat oil in heavy large saucepan over medium-high heat. Add beef; cook until brown, crumbling with spoon, about 4 minutes. Add onion, bell pepper and garlic and sauté until onion is translucent, about 5 minutes. Reduce heat to medium-low. Add tomatoes with their juices and next 10 ingredients. Cover; simmer until slightly thickened, about 20 minutes. Season with salt and pepper. *(Can be made 1 day ahead; chill. Rewarm over medium-low heat.)*
• Transfer mixture to large bowl or chafing dish and sprinkle with almonds. Serve with tortilla chips.
• *6 servings*

Clockwise from top left:
Fiesta Chicken Salad with
Lime-Cilantro Vinaigrette;
Picadillo with tortilla chips;
Pico de Gallo

Pico de Gallo

Offer this fresh salsa with tortilla chips as an additional appetizer. It's also perfect with the cheese enchiladas.

2 1/4   pounds plum tomatoes, seeded, finely chopped
   1   large onion, finely chopped
  3/4   cup chopped fresh cilantro
   5   garlic cloves, minced
   3   jalapeño chilies, seeded, minced
   3   tablespoons fresh lime juice

• Combine all ingredients in bowl. Season with salt and pepper. Cover; chill at least 1 hour and up to 4 hours before serving.
• *Makes about 5 cups*

Cheese Enchiladas with Green Sauce

Spinach, green onions, cilantro and chilies give the sauce its name—and lots of flavor.

SAUCE
  1/2   10-ounce package frozen chopped spinach
   1   tablespoon butter
   1   tablespoon all purpose flour
   1   cup whipping cream
   1   cup milk
   6   tablespoons chopped fresh cilantro
   3   green onions, minced
  1/2   4-ounce can diced green chilies, drained
1 3/4   teaspoons ground cumin
1 1/2   teaspoons ground coriander
  1/4   teaspoon dried crushed red pepper

ENCHILADAS
  1/2   cup vegetable oil
  12   6-inch corn tortillas
   3   cups grated mild cheddar cheese
1 1/2   cups grated Monterey Jack cheese
  1/2   cup finely chopped onion
   1   tablespoon chopped fresh cilantro

  1/2   cup sour cream

• FOR SAUCE: Cook spinach according to package instructions. Drain well. Set aside. Melt butter in heavy medium skillet over medium heat. Add flour and stir mixture 2 minutes; do not brown. Gradually whisk in whipping cream and milk. Simmer until thickened, about 5 minutes. Stir in spinach, cilantro, green onions, chilies, cumin, coriander and red pepper. Puree in batches in processor until almost smooth. Season with salt and pepper. *(Can be prepared 1 day ahead. Cover and refrigerate. Bring to room temperature before using.)*
• FOR ENCHILADAS: Heat oil in heavy small skillet over medium-high heat. Using tongs, briefly dip each tortilla in oil to soften, about 15 seconds per side. Transfer to paper towels and drain. Combine cheeses in large bowl; set aside 1½ cups for topping. Combine onion and cilantro in small bowl. Place ¼ cup cheese mixture in center of 1 tortilla. Spoon 2 teaspoons onion mixture over. Roll up tortilla. Place seam side down in large glass baking dish. Repeat with remaining tortillas, cheese and onion, using ¼ cup cheese for each. *(Can be made 1 day ahead. Cover and chill.)*
• Preheat oven to 375°F. Stir sour cream into sauce; pour over enchiladas. Sprinkle with reserved 1½ cups cheese. Bake until cheese melts and enchiladas are heated through, about 25 minutes. Serve hot.
• *6 servings*

"Drunken" Beans

Called *frijoles borrachos* in Mexico, these beans are accented with dark beer.

- 8 bacon slices, cut into 1-inch pieces

- 1 pound dried pinto beans
- 5 1/2 cups water
- 2 onions, chopped
- 8 large garlic cloves, minced
- 1 12-ounce bottle dark beer
- 4 teaspoons ground cumin
- 1 tablespoon ground coriander
- 1 tablespoon sugar
- 1 tablespoon chili powder
- 1 jalapeño chili, chopped

- 3 plum tomatoes, chopped
- 1 cup chopped fresh cilantro

• Cook bacon in heavy large pot over medium-high heat until brown and almost crisp. Using slotted spoon, transfer to paper towels and drain; discard drippings. Return bacon to same large pot.
• Place beans in same pot. Add water, onions and garlic; boil 15 minutes. Reduce heat to medium. Add beer, cumin, coriander, sugar, chili powder and jalapeño. Cover partially and simmer 1 hour.
• Add tomatoes to beans, cover partially and simmer 45 minutes. Uncover; simmer until beans are tender and mixture is thick, about 20 minutes. *(Can be made 1 day ahead. Cover; chill. Bring to simmer before serving.)* Stir cilantro into beans. Season with salt and pepper and serve.

• *6 servings*

Fiesta Chicken Salad with Lime-Cilantro Vinaigrette

VINAIGRETTE
- 1/2 cup chopped shallots
- 1/4 cup fresh lime juice
- 1/4 cup chopped fresh cilantro
- 1 tablespoon minced garlic
- 1/2 cup vegetable oil

SALAD
- 3 cups thinly sliced red leaf lettuce
- 3 cups thinly sliced Napa cabbage
- 1 cup diced cooked chicken breast
- 2 plum tomatoes, seeded, chopped
- 1/2 red bell pepper, thinly sliced
- 1/2 yellow bell pepper, thinly sliced
- 1/2 avocado, peeled, diced
- 1/3 cup crumbled tortilla chips
- 1/4 cup cooked fresh corn kernels or frozen, thawed
- 1/4 cup pumpkin seeds,* toasted
- 1/4 cup thinly sliced onion
- 1/2 cup crumbled queso añejo** or feta cheese (about 2 ounces)

• FOR VINAIGRETTE: Combine first 4 ingredients in medium bowl. Gradually whisk in oil. Season with salt and pepper. *(Can be made 1 day ahead. Cover and chill. Bring to room temperature before using.)*
• FOR SALAD: Combine all ingredients except cheese in large bowl. Toss with vinaigrette to coat. Top with cheese.
*Also known as pepitas. *Available at Latin American markets, natural foods stores and many supermarkets.*
**Queso añejo *is a dry, white, aged cheese available at Latin American markets.*

• *6 servings*

Mexican Chocolate Cake

2	cups sugar
1 3/4	cups all purpose flour
2	teaspoons ground cinnamon
1	teaspoon baking soda
1/4	teaspoon salt
1 1/2	cups buttermilk
1	cup (2 sticks) unsalted butter
3/4	cup unsweetened cocoa powder
2	large eggs, beaten to blend
1 1/2	teaspoons vanilla extract
	Mocha Frosting (see recipe at right)
2	cups chopped toasted pecans

• Preheat oven to 350°F. Butter and flour 13 x 9 x 2-inch baking pan. Combine sugar, flour, ground cinnamon, baking soda and salt in large bowl. Whisk buttermilk, butter and cocoa powder in heavy large saucepan over medium-low heat until butter melts. Pour over flour mixture and whisk to combine. Add eggs and vanilla; whisk to blend. Pour into pan. Bake until tester inserted into center comes out clean, about 40 minutes. Transfer to rack and cool completely.

• Run knife around pan sides to loosen cake. Turn out cake onto platter. Spread frosting over top and sides of cake. Press enough pecans onto sides of cake to cover. Sprinkle cake with remaining pecans. *(Can be made 1 day ahead. Cover; let stand at room temperature.)*

• *12 servings*

Mocha Frosting

1/2	cup (1 stick) unsalted butter
1/2	cup unsweetened cocoa powder
6	tablespoons buttermilk
1 1/2	teaspoons instant espresso powder
1 1/2	teaspoons vanilla extract
1/2	teaspoon ground cinnamon
1	1-pound box powdered sugar

• Melt butter in medium saucepan over medium heat. Add cocoa, buttermilk, espresso powder, vanilla and cinnamon; whisk until smooth. Remove from heat. Place powdered sugar in bowl. Pour hot cocoa mixture over. Using electric mixer, beat until smooth. Use frosting immediately.

• *Makes about 2 cups*

Cheese Enchiladas with Green Sauce; Fiesta Chicken Salad with Lime-Cilantro Vinaigrette; "Drunken" Beans

garden party

Dinner for Eight

- Cheese Quesadillas with Salsa Verde

- Margaritas

- Baked Striped Bass with Tomatoes

- Mixed Greens with Raspberry Vinaigrette

- Grilled Chili Corn

- Basil, Rosemary and Tomato Focaccia

- Chardonnay

- Nectarine and Raspberry Crostata with Vanilla Crème Fraîche

In summer, when back-yard gardens swell with fruits and vegetables ripe for the picking and farmers' markets fill with local harvests, the baskets and bushels of produce that find their way to your kitchen are reasons enough for a party. Corn, tomatoes, herbs, lettuces, nectarines and raspberries—with ingredients like these at their best, dinner can't help but be delicious. ★ These recipes frame the season's best. The delicacy of the fish you went down to the docks to buy—or maybe caught yourself—marries well with a simple salad of tomatoes and herbs. Young lettuces need only a splash of raspberry-

mustard vinaigrette. Ears of corn, brushed with a chili-lime marinade, grill to tenderness in minutes.

★ From Italy, where an appreciation for fresh produce reigns, come two baked specialties. First there is garlicky *focaccia* bread blanketed with tomatoes and herbs (above right). And then there is a free-form tart, called a *crostata*, that bubbles over with the juices of nectarines and raspberries. ★ This is the kind of food you want to take outdoors—out onto the porch or balcony, to the back yard or, maybe, to a table set up in the garden where many of the meal's ingredients were growing just hours before.

Seasonal Bests

To expand the Garden Party menu, or as alternatives to the recipes included, here are ideas for showcasing summer's best tastes in easy preparations.

Melon and prosciutto: Wrap ribbons of prosciutto around wedges of ripe honeydew or cantaloupe.

Sliced tomatoes: Arrange overlapping concentric circles of ripe tomatoes, either red or red and yellow, on a big platter and drizzle lightly with equal parts olive oil and balsamic vinegar. Sprinkle with a julienne of fresh basil.

Grilled summer squash: Cut small zucchini and yellow squash in half lengthwise; brush cut sides with equal parts olive oil and balsamic vinegar. Grill skin-side down for 10 minutes; turn and continue grilling until tender, 5 to 10 minutes more. Bell peppers can be grilled the same way. Brush both sides of halved peppers with oil and vinegar and grill 20 to 25 minutes.

Mixed nectarines and berries: Make the filling for the *crostata* as directed in the recipe, and serve it with the Vanilla Crème Fraîche or whipped cream.

Peaches and cream: Slice ripe peaches into dessert bowls. Top with sour cream flavored with amaretto, sugar and cinnamon. Sprinkle the dessert with toasted sliced almonds.

Melon with liqueur and sorbet: Sprinkle honeydew chunks lightly with Midori liqueur and lemon juice; serve with raspberry sorbet. Blueberries can be prepared the same way, sprinkled with crème de cassis and lemon juice and served with strawberry sorbet.

Cheese Quesadillas with Salsa Verde

Crispy corn tortillas filled with Monterey Jack cheese and paired with a tomatillo salsa are an easy starter for this outdoor party.

    8   teaspoons (about) vegetable oil
   16   6-inch corn tortillas
    2   cups shredded Monterey Jack
        cheese (about 8 ounces)

        Salsa Verde (see recipe below)

• Heat 1 teaspoon oil in medium nonstick skillet over medium-high heat. Add 1 tortilla. Sprinkle tortilla with ¼ cup cheese. Top with another tortilla and press with spatula to compact. Cook until cheese melts and tortillas are crisp and light golden, about 2 minutes per side. Transfer to work surface. Repeat with remaining tortillas and cheese, adding more oil by teaspoonfuls as necessary.
• Cut quesadillas into quarters; place on platter. Serve with Salsa Verde.
• *Makes 8*

Salsa Verde

    2   pounds fresh tomatillos,*
        husked, chopped
    2   small onions, chopped
    1   cup water

    1   cup chopped fresh cilantro
    4   jalapeño chilies, seeded, minced
    2   garlic cloves, minced

• Combine tomatillos, onions and water in heavy large saucepan. Boil until tomatillos are tender, stirring occasionally, about 5 minutes. Transfer mixture to processor; process until chunky puree forms. Chill until cool, about 1 hour. *(Can be made 1 day ahead. Cover and keep chilled.)*
• Stir cilantro, chilies and garlic into salsa. Season to taste with salt.
A green tomato-like vegetable with a paper-thin husk. Available at Latin American markets and some supermarkets.
• *Makes about 4 cups*

Clockwise from top left: Grilled Chili Corn; Baked Striped Bass with Tomatoes; Margarita

Baked Striped Bass with Tomatoes

Whole bass stuffed with cilantro and surrounded by cherry tomatoes make an impressive presentation.

3/4	cup plus 3 tablespoons olive oil
6	tablespoons balsamic vinegar
2	tablespoons chopped fresh cilantro
2	tablespoons chopped fresh basil or 2 teaspoons dried
2	1-pint baskets cherry tomatoes, halved

3	2-pound whole striped bass, cleaned, heads and tails left intact
3	tablespoons fresh lemon juice
3	tablespoons coarse salt
2	bunches cilantro sprigs, trimmed
10	shallots, chopped

• Whisk ¾ cup oil and vinegar in medium bowl to blend. Stir in chopped cilantro and basil. Season with salt and pepper. Mix tomatoes into dressing. *(Tomato mixture can be made 2 hours ahead. Let stand at room temperature.)*
• Preheat oven to 350°F. Place fish on large baking sheet. Rub inside of each fish with 1 tablespoon lemon juice and ½ tablespoon coarse salt. Stuff cavities with cilantro sprigs and shallots, dividing equally among fish. Sprinkle each fish with ½ tablespoon coarse salt, then 1 tablespoon olive oil.
• Bake fish until just opaque in center, about 30 minutes. Transfer to large platter. Spoon tomato mixture around fish and serve.

• *8 servings*

Mixed Greens with Raspberry Vinaigrette

3	tablespoons raspberry vinegar
1	tablespoon Dijon mustard
1	teaspoon minced garlic
1/2	teaspoon anchovy paste
1/3	cup olive oil

8	cups mixed baby greens (about 7 ounces)
2	bunches arugula

• Combine first 4 ingredients in medium bowl. Gradually whisk in olive oil. Season to taste with salt and pepper.
• Combine mixed baby greens and arugula in large bowl. Toss with enough dressing to coat and serve immediately.

• *8 servings*

Grilled Chili Corn

1/2	cup olive oil
1/4	cup fresh lime juice
2	tablespoons chili powder
1	teaspoon dried crushed red pepper
12	ears corn, husked

1/2	cup (1 stick) butter, melted

• Prepare barbecue (medium-high heat). Combine first 4 ingredients in large bowl and whisk to blend. Season generously with salt. Place corn in large baking dish. Rub all of oil mixture over corn, covering completely.
• Grill corn until tender, basting frequently with melted butter and any oil mixture from bottom of baking dish and turning frequently, about 10 minutes. Transfer to platter.

• *8 servings*

Cheese Quesadillas
with Salsa Verde

Basil, Rosemary and Tomato Focaccia

Here, fresh-from-the-garden tomatoes and herbs top a delicious Italian bread. Accompany with the extra garlic oil.

3/4 cup olive oil
6 garlic cloves, minced
3/4 teaspoon dried crushed red pepper

2 cups warm water (105°F to 115°F)
1 envelope dry yeast
5 cups (about) unbleached all purpose flour
2 teaspoons salt

8 medium-size plum tomatoes, seeded, cut into 1-inch pieces
2 tablespoons coarse salt

2 tablespoons chopped fresh rosemary
2 tablespoons thinly sliced fresh basil

• Combine oil, garlic and crushed red pepper in heavy small saucepan. Stir over medium-low heat until garlic is golden, about 5 minutes. Remove from heat and let stand at least 1 hour. *(Can be prepared 1 day ahead. Cover and refrigerate. Bring to room temperature before using.)*

• Pour 2 cups warm water into large glass measuring cup. Sprinkle yeast over and let stand until yeast dissolves, about 10 minutes. Whisk in 3 tablespoons garlic oil. Combine 2 cups flour and 2 teaspoons salt in bowl of heavy-duty mixer. Add yeast mixture and beat until incorporated. Mix in enough remaining flour 1 cup at a time to form soft dough. Beat on low speed just until dough is smooth, approximately 3 minutes.

• Brush large bowl with 1 tablespoon garlic oil. Transfer dough to prepared bowl. Turn to coat with oil. Cover with plastic, then damp kitchen towel. Let dough rise in warm draft-free area until doubled in volume, about 1 hour.

• Place tomatoes in colander set over large bowl. Toss with 1 tablespoon coarse salt. Let stand 15 minutes. Rinse under cold water. Transfer tomatoes to paper towels; drain well.

• Preheat oven to 450°F. Brush 15 x 10 x 1-inch baking sheet with 1 tablespoon garlic oil. Punch down dough. Knead briefly in bowl. Transfer dough to prepared sheet. Using oiled hands, stretch dough to roughly fit pan. Press dough all over with fingertips to dimple. Sprinkle dough with rosemary, then tomatoes, pressing some into dimples. Sprinkle with basil and remaining 1 tablespoon coarse salt.

• Bake focaccia until golden brown, about 30 minutes. Transfer to rack. Cool. Cut focaccia into squares. Serve with remaining garlic oil.

• *Makes 1 focaccia*

Nectarine and Raspberry Crostata with Vanilla Crème Fraîche

This Italian-style, free-form tart has buttery pastry and lots of fresh fruit.

     2   cups all purpose flour
    1/4   cup sugar
    1/2   teaspoon salt
     1   cup (2 sticks) chilled unsalted butter
     2   tablespoons (about) ice water

     1   1/2-pint basket raspberries
     4   nectarines (about 1 1/4 pounds), pitted, thinly sliced
    1/3   cup plus 2 tablespoons sugar
     1   tablespoon fresh lemon juice
     1   egg, beaten to blend

          Vanilla Crème Fraîche
          (see recipe at right)

• Mix flour, ¼ cup sugar and salt in processor. Add butter; using on/off turns, process until mixture resembles coarse meal. Add water by tablespoonfuls and process just until moist clumps form. Gather dough into ball. Flatten into disk. Wrap in plastic and chill at least 1 hour. (Can be made 1 day ahead. Keep chilled. Let soften slightly before rolling.)

• Preheat oven to 375°F. Roll out dough on lightly floured parchment paper to ¼-inch-thick round. Trim dough to 14-inch round. Transfer parchment with dough to large baking sheet. Mash ½ cup raspberries in large bowl. Add remaining raspberries, nectarines, ⅓ cup sugar and lemon juice; toss to coat. Spoon mixture into center of dough, leaving 3-inch border. Sprinkle fruit with 2 tablespoons sugar. Fold border over fruit, pinching to seal any cracks. Brush dough with some of beaten egg.

• Bake crostata until pastry is golden brown and filling bubbles, about 35 minutes. Transfer sheet to rack and cool slightly.

• Serve crostata warm or at room temperature with Vanilla Crème Fraîche.

• *8 servings*

Vanilla Crème Fraîche

     1   8-ounce container crème fraîche or sour cream
    1/2   vanilla bean, split lengthwise
    4 1/2 teaspoons sugar

• Place crème fraîche in medium bowl. Scrape seeds from vanilla bean into crème fraîche. Stir in sugar. Cover; refrigerate 1 hour. *(Can be prepared 3 days ahead. Keep refrigerated.)*

• *Makes about 1 cup*

Nectarine and Raspberry Crostata with Vanilla Crème Fraîche

mix-and-match recipes

It would be hard to find a party menu that didn't get changed at least a few times between the initial inspiration and the actual cooking. There are always factors that call for some juggling—maybe the peppers in the market don't look all that good; your friend's new romantic interest is allergic to seafood; the weatherman's predicting rain; or the dessert just has to be chocolate. ★ So just as the menus in the first part of this book invite party planning and promise delectable meals, the recipes in the following sections address the inevitable need to tinker with those menus and make substitutions that will work just as well. ★ Each recipe, be it an appetizer, soup, salad, side dish, main course or dessert, comes with a note suggesting which dish in which menu it might replace. There are many options for each party. For example, if you like the idea of "Dinner and a Movie," but a guest's allergy means you have to serve something other than the scampi main course, you will find two chicken dishes, a lamb stew and a pasta designated as possible alternatives. Similarly, if the season is great for a picnic but not so good for asparagus, you'll find other good travelers for the "Picnic in the Country" among the salads and side dishes. ★ Use these recipes to fine-tune a menu to fit your schedule, too. If you'd like to prepare dessert a day or two before the "Back-Yard Barbecue," for example, choose a frozen dessert instead of the sabayon on the menu. If you don't have the time to make all the individual hors d'oeuvres for "Cocktails at Five," browse through the appetizers section for choices such as Caviar Pie that come together faster. ★ Guest lists have a way of outgrowing the best-laid menu plans. Sometimes the easiest way to stretch a menu is to double the main course recipe and fill in with additional side dishes, then finish with a "bigger" dessert. When the meal isn't a sit-down,

you can add another entrée, or even two, and serve smaller portions of everything. This strategy

would certainly succeed in the "Pasta Party," the "Picnic in the Country" and "Cocktails at Five,"

with the add-on for another two or three guests being, respectively, a pasta recipe, a portable salad and

an appetizer or dip. ★ And then there's the possibility that you'll find a recipe in the pages that follow that you

just have to make—and it becomes the start of a party you shape and create. It may be a chocolate layer cake so

luscious you just want to get into the kitchen and bake, or a pasta that sounds irresistible, or salsa- and guacamole-

topped fajitas that put you in the mood for Mexican food. As you plan your own menu, turn to those in the

front of the book for inspiration, if you like, substituting that cake for, say, the

chocolate tart in "Dinner in the Kitchen." Or set out on your own, using

the advice on page 136 as a guide and combining recipes to create the

exact menu you want to make. ★ Finally, in an effort to cover every

entertaining "base," we've included four "generic" menus in the back of

the book, which are designed to bend to the occasion that already has a

theme, and a reason to be. For instance, you know you will be celebrating a

relative's birthday next month, and that you'd like to do something outside. Maybe The Cookout menu will do. Or,

you've invited friends to stop by your house after you all go to the ballet in a couple of weeks, and now you need to

decide what to offer them. Perhaps The Dessert Buffet would be just right at the end of the evening. The

idea is that these versatile menus are just what's needed for the kind of parties we all have all

year long—whatever the occasion. ★ And versatility is really what the last half of this book

is about, with recipes that will mix and match to suit the menu you have in mind, and

hand-holding guidance in the form of suggestions, menus and sidebars filled with advice.

The perfect party was never so easy.

Top to bottom: Fettuccine with Garlic Shrimp and Basil-Mint Pesto (page 40); Spinach and Cheese-stuffed Pasta Shells (page 147); Penne with Sausage, Peas and Mascarpone (page 145)

Easy Guacamole

For a family larger than the one figured into the menu for the Family Reunion (page 64), throw a big fajita party, one that begins with this simple guacamole recipe and includes the Jalapeño Cheese Squares on page 103, Fiesta Fajitas on page 139, stewed beans, a mixed fruit salad and the Vanilla Flan with Raspberries on page 163. This recipe makes enough guacamole to serve as a dip with chips and as a topping for the fajitas.

15	ripe avocados, halved, pitted, peeled
1 1/2	cups purchased medium-hot salsa
2	tablespoons buttermilk ranch-style salad dressing mix
	Tortilla chips

• Place avocados in large bowl and mash coarsely. Stir in salsa and buttermilk dressing mix. *(Can be prepared 2 hours ahead. Press plastic wrap onto surface of guacamole and refrigerate.)* Serve guacamole with tortilla chips.
• *Makes about 12 cups*

Garlicky Eggplant Spread

This delicious, do-ahead eggplant spread, which gets served with wedges of pita bread, would make a good appetizer for the Dinner in the Kitchen menu (page 10).

2	large eggplants (about 2 1/2 pounds)
2	large garlic cloves, slivered
1/4	cup olive oil
2	tablespoons fresh lemon juice
2	tablespoons chopped fresh oregano or 2 teaspoons dried
1	teaspoon ground cumin
	Red leaf lettuce
4	tomatoes, sliced
	Pita bread
	Chopped fresh oregano

• Preheat oven to 450°F. Cut slits in eggplants with tip of knife and insert garlic sliver into each slit. Place eggplants in baking pan and bake until very tender, about 1 hour. Cut each eggplant in half and cool slightly.
• Scrape eggplant pulp from skin into colander and let drain. Transfer eggplant to processor. Add oil, lemon juice, 2 tablespoons oregano and cumin. Puree until smooth. Season with salt and pepper. Cool completely. *(Can be prepared 1 day ahead. Cover and refrigerate.)*
• Line platter with lettuce. Halve tomato slices and arrange around edge of platter. Cut pita into wedges and arrange around platter. Mound eggplant mixture in center. Sprinkle with oregano.
• *6 to 8 servings*

102

mix-and-match appetizers

Glass Act

There is a glass for every beverage. Tall flutes are designed to hold in Champagne bubbles. Wide-bowled red wine glasses maximize exposure to the bouquet of a French Burgundy. To name just two. Buy what you like, then feel free to use them for other than their intended purposes. Read on for different ideas.

All purpose wine glasses: Their large bowls (about 12 ounces) make these appropriate for red wines as well as white. (Red wine should not fill more than half a glass, to allow "breathing" room.) They can double as water goblets and dessert dishes for scoops of sorbet or a chilled mousse garnished with fresh berries.

Highballs: These tall, elegant glasses are especially versatile, serving up a gin and tonic as nicely as iced tea. You can also use them as water glasses, or even to hold breadsticks on the table.

Tumblers: Short and squat, these can be used for mixed drinks, with or without ice. When the meal is casual, it can be kind of romantic to drink red wine from the small ones. And the larger ones can take a scoop or two of ice cream when it comes to dessert.

Flutes: Champagne flutes or tulips (so named because they are shaped like closed tulips) make everyone feel elegant, and make even an inexpensive bottle of sparkling wine a little special. Try using them as bud vases, grouped together as a centerpiece.

Aperitif glasses: These come in a variety of sizes and go by a number of names, from hocks to cordials. They are small stemmed glasses, and can be used to hold a Martini, an aperitif, Champagne, a dessert wine—or dessert, actually, like a thick chocolate mousse.

Snifters: Intended for brandy, these can make any kind of after-dinner drink dramatic. They'll do double-duty as ice cream bowls (drizzle with liqueur) or small vases to hold a single floating blossom.

Jalapeño Cheese Squares

Include these in the Fajita Party menu (see the Easy Guacamole recipe on page 102 for details).

10	large eggs
1/4	cup minced fresh jalapeño chilies
2	tablespoons chili powder
4	teaspoons ground cumin
1 1/2	cups milk (do not use lowfat or nonfat)
4	cups grated Monterey Jack cheese (about 1 pound)
2	cups chopped green onions (about 12)
4	cups grated cheddar cheese (about 1 pound)

• Preheat oven to 350°F. Butter two 9-inch square glass baking dishes. Whisk first 4 ingredients in large bowl to blend. Whisk in milk. Add Monterey Jack cheese and onions and stir to combine. Divide mixture between prepared dishes. Sprinkle half of cheddar cheese over each dish. Bake until tops are light brown and puffed, about 45 minutes. Cool slightly. Cut into 1½-inch squares. *(Can be prepared 8 hours ahead. Transfer squares to heavy large cookie sheet. Cover and refrigerate. Before serving, rewarm in 350°F oven until heated through, about 10 minutes.)* Transfer cheese squares to platter and serve.

• *Makes about 72 squares*

Crab and Avocado "Sushi" with Soy Dipping Sauce

A clever and elegant appetizer that would work well in the cocktail party menu (page 18), replacing the crab and corn salad in endive spears.

SUSHI

6	8-inch-diameter rice paper sheets*
1 1/2	cups (about) mung bean sprouts
1 1/2	cups fresh crabmeat
1 1/2	(about) large avocados, peeled, halved, pitted, cut into 1/2-inch-thick slices
6	tablespoons minced fresh cilantro

SAUCE

1/4	cup rice vinegar
2	tablespoons soy sauce
1	teaspoon sugar
1/2	teaspoon wasabi powder* mixed with 1/2 teaspoon water
1/2	teaspoon minced fresh ginger

• FOR SUSHI: Fill large bowl with hot water. Quickly dip 1 rice paper sheet into water. Place rice paper on wet kitchen towel. Let rest 30 seconds so that rice paper becomes soft and pliable (if rice paper is still stiff, sprinkle more hot water over).

• Starting 2 inches in from bottom, place ¼ cup bean sprouts in 1-inch-wide strip across width of rice paper, leaving 1-inch border on sides. Top sprouts with ¼ cup crabmeat, then 2 avocado slices and 1 tablespoon minced fresh cilantro. Fold 2-inch bottom border of rice paper over filling. Fold in sides. Roll up tightly jelly roll style. Place seam side down on plate. Repeat with remaining rice paper sheets, sprouts, crabmeat, avocado and cilantro. Cover and refrigerate rolls at least 1 and up to 6 hours.

• FOR SAUCE: Mix all ingredients in small bowl to blend.

• Cut rolls crosswise into 1½-inch-long pieces. Stand rolls up on ends. Serve with dipping sauce.

Rice paper sheets and wasabi (horseradish powder) are available at Japanese markets and some supermarkets.

• *8 to 10 servings*

Crab and Avocado "Sushi"
with Soy Dipping Sauce

Brie and Chive Fondue

This version of the classic dish uses Brie instead of Swiss cheese and fresh grapefruit juice to replace the wine. Serve with pumpernickel, sourdough or rye bread cubes. Cooked shrimp, blanched asparagus spears, Belgian endive leaves and boiled baby red potatoes are all good "dippers" too. Offer this appetizer in place of the tomato and cheese tart in the Bistro Supper menu (page 42).

1	pound chilled slightly firm Brie cheese
1	tablespoon all purpose flour
1 1/2	teaspoons unsalted butter
4 1/2	teaspoons minced shallots
3/4	cup (or more) fresh pink grapefruit juice
	White pepper
2	tablespoons chopped fresh chives
1/2	teaspoon minced grapefruit peel
	Pumpernickel, sourdough or rye bread, cut into 1-inch cubes

• Remove rind from cheese. Tear cheese into pieces and place in large bowl. Add flour and toss to coat.
• Melt butter in heavy medium saucepan over medium heat. Add shallots and sauté until golden brown, 4 minutes. Add ¾ cup grapefruit juice. Simmer until reduced to ½ cup, 7 minutes. Reduce heat to medium-low.
• Add 1 handful Brie to saucepan and stir constantly until cheese melts, about 5 minutes. Repeat with remaining cheese, 1 handful at a time. Season to taste with white pepper. *(Can be prepared 1 day ahead. Cover and refrigerate. Reheat over low heat, stirring frequently. Thin with more juice if needed.)* Stir in chives and grapefruit peel.
• Pour cheese mixture into fondue pot. Set pot over candle or canned heat. Serve with skewers of bread cubes.
• *Makes about 2 cups*

Black Bean and Garbanzo Bean Hummus

This unique dip is a blend of garbanzo beans, tahini and black beans, flavored with garlic and lime juice. Serve it with triangles of pita bread during the Cocktails at Five party (page 18).

2	15- to 16-ounce cans garbanzo beans (chickpeas)
1/3	cup tahini (sesame seed paste)*
1/3	cup fresh lime juice
4	teaspoons chopped fresh garlic
1	15- to 16-ounce can black beans, rinsed, drained well
	Pinch of cayenne pepper
	Pita bread, cut into triangles

• Drain garbanzo beans, reserving ½ cup liquid. Rinse garbanzo beans; drain well. Combine garbanzo beans, tahini, lime juice and garlic in processor and puree until smooth. Add black beans and process just until beans are coarsely chopped. Transfer to large bowl. Stir in enough reserved liquid from garbanzo beans to thin mixture to consistency of thick mayonnaise. Add cayenne pepper. Season with salt and pepper. *(Can be prepared 1 day ahead. Cover and refrigerate.)* Serve with pita bread.
* *Available at Middle Eastern and natural foods stores and some supermarkets.*
• *Makes about 4 cups*

Crab-stuffed Jalapeño Fritters

Add a Latin touch to the eclectic mix of cuisines represented in the cocktail party (page 18) with these spicy stuffed chilies.

12	large jalapeños
4	ounces crabmeat, well drained
1/3	cup minced red onion
1/4	cup minced green bell pepper
1/4	cup mayonnaise
1/2	cup all purpose flour
3/4	cup Mexican beer
	Corn oil (for deep frying)
	All purpose flour
1/2	avocado, peeled, diced
1/2	cup mild salsa, drained
1	tablespoon mayonnaise

• Starting just below stem, cut chilies lengthwise in half, leaving stems attached. Seed chilies. Place chilies in heavy medium saucepan. Cover with cold water and bring to simmer. Drain. Repeat process. Dry chilies.
• Combine crab, onion, bell pepper and mayonnaise in small bowl. Season with salt and pepper. Fill chili cavities with crab mixture. Press chili halves together to compress filling. *(Can be prepared 4 hours ahead. Cover and chill.)*
• Place ½ cup flour in bowl. Gradually whisk in beer. Let stand 30 minutes.
• Heat oil in heavy deep pot to 375°F. Whisk batter to smooth. Dredge jalapeños in flour. Holding stem end, dip into batter to coat completely and deep-fry in batches until golden brown, about 3 minutes. Using slotted spoon, transfer jalapeños to paper towels and drain. Combine avocado, salsa and mayonnaise in small bowl. Season to taste. Arrange chilies on platter. Garnish with salsa.
• *Makes 12*

Spicy Shrimp Cocktail with Tomato and Cilantro

A new take on the classic appetizer, this one heated by the bite of chilies. Make it up to a day ahead, and serve it at the start of the South-of-the-Border Party (page 84).

1	cup tomato juice
1/2	cup bottled clam juice
1/4	cup Sherry wine vinegar
10	large cilantro sprigs
1	serrano chili or jalapeño chili, cut in half
1 1/2	teaspoons Worcestershire sauce
1 1/2	teaspoons olive oil
1	pound uncooked large shrimp, peeled, deveined
1/2	large tomato, chopped
1	green onion, chopped
1	tablespoon chopped fresh cilantro
1/2	teaspoon fresh lime juice
1/2	teaspoon sugar
	Lime wedges

• Combine tomato juice, clam juice, vinegar, cilantro sprigs, chilies and Worcestershire sauce in small saucepan. Boil until sauce is slightly thickened and reduced to 1 cup, about 20 minutes. Strain into medium bowl.

• Heat oil in large nonstick skillet over medium-high heat. Add shrimp and sauté until just cooked through, about 4 minutes. Cool shrimp.

• Add shrimp, tomato, green onion, chopped cilantro, lime juice and sugar to sauce. Season with salt and pepper. Chill until cold, at least 3 hours. *(Can be made 1 day ahead. Cover and keep chilled.)* Garnish with lime wedges.

• *6 servings*

Serving Up Style

Style can be about taking something out of its "proper" place and using it in unexpected ways. This works in fashion, and it works at the table, with serving pieces especially. Try these ideas, and then let them inspire your own.

Small tongs, the kind originally designed for ice or olives, make tidy servers for sliced meats, green beans and asparagus, as well as some hors d'oeuvres, like spring rolls.

Soup ladles do double duty in punch bowls; use the small ones for dessert sauces and toppings.

Butter spreaders are just right for soft cheeses, pâtés, appetizer mousses and savory spreads.

Pie servers give guests a handle on mini pizzas and other appetizers, as well as sliced tomatoes and grilled onions.

Little relish forks are handy for spearing shrimp, smoked salmon and chunks of pineapple and melon.

Demitasse spoons can deliver just the right drizzle or dab of salsa, mustard, relish or caviar.

Small wooden scoops invite guests to help themselves to olives, cocktail onions, nuts or candies.

Painted chopsticks make clever servers for sushi, cold cuts, shrimp and anything else that's easy to grasp.

Classic Bloody Marys

Tying the vegetable garnish in a bundle adds an elegant touch to these cocktails, which might make an eye-opening start to the Lunch on the Terrace menu (page 28; halve the recipe). These also star in The Brunch menu on page 112.

8 cups tomato juice or vegetable juice
2 tablespoons prepared horseradish
2 tablespoons fresh lemon juice
1 tablespoon celery salt
2 teaspoons Worcestershire sauce
1 teaspoon hot pepper sauce (such as Tabasco)

8 celery stalks with leaves
4 carrots, peeled, halved lengthwise
1 cucumber, cut lengthwise into 8 strips
4 green onion tops (dark green parts only), cut lengthwise into long strips

Ice cubes
1 1/2 cups vodka

• Mix first 6 ingredients in large pitcher. Season to taste with pepper. Cover and chill until cold, about 1 hour. *(Can be prepared 1 day ahead. Keep refrigerated.)*
• Tie 1 celery stalk, 1 carrot stick and 1 cucumber strip together into bundle using green onion top. Repeat with remaining celery, carrots, cucumber and green onion tops. *(Can be prepared 8 hours ahead. Cover and refrigerate.)*
• Fill tall glasses with ice. Mix vodka into tomato mixture. Pour into glasses. Garnish with vegetable bundles.
• *8 servings*

Crudités and Grilled Sausages with Sweet and Hot Chutneys

More interesting—much—than chips and dip, but not much more work. For a cocktail party, like the one on page 18, make the chutneys ahead, then grill the sausages just before serving. These also make a great appetizer in The Potluck menu on page 126.

Vegetables to dip (such as carrot sticks, steamed broccoli florets, jicama and cauliflower)
3 pounds fully cooked sausages (such as bratwurst and kielbasa)
Sweet Chutney (see recipe at right)
Hot Chutney (see recipe at right)

• Arrange vegetables around edge of platter. Grill or panfry sausages until brown and heated through. Cut into 1-inch pieces. Arrange sausage pieces in center of platter, placing toothpick in each piece. Serve with chutneys.
• *12 servings*

Sweet Chutney

1 cup mayonnaise or low-fat mayonnaise
2/3 cup Major Grey mango chutney
1 teaspoon curry powder
1/4 teaspoon cayenne pepper

• Blend all ingredients in processor. Transfer to bowl. *(Can be prepared 2 days ahead. Cover and refrigerate.)*
• *Makes about 1 ½ cups*

Hot Chutney

2 cups (packed) fresh mint leaves
2 cups (packed) fresh cilantro leaves
2/3 cup cider vinegar
1/4 cup sugar
4 jalapeño chilies, seeded
1 2-inch fresh ginger piece, peeled, cut into 1/2-inch pieces
1 teaspoon salt
1/2 cup plain yogurt

• Combine all ingredients except yogurt in processor and blend until very finely chopped. Mix in yogurt. Transfer to bowl. *(Can be prepared 1 day ahead. Cover chutney and refrigerate.)*
• *Makes about 2 cups*

Classic Bloody Marys

Roasted Portobello Mushrooms with Fontina

A different treatment for those delicious portobello mushrooms that turn up in the Pasta Party (page 34).

3 tablespoons olive oil
2 tablespoons chopped fresh basil
2 tablespoons chopped fresh parsley
3 garlic cloves, minced
6 4- to 5-inch-diameter portobello mushrooms, stems removed

12 ounces Fontina cheese, cut into 3 x 1/2 x 1/2-inch strips
6 slices bread from crusty round loaf, lightly toasted

• Position oven rack 6 inches from broiler. Preheat broiler. Mix first 4 ingredients in bowl. Place mushrooms, stem side up, on heavy large baking sheet. Brush with oil mixture. Season with salt and pepper. Broil mushrooms until just cooked through, about 3 minutes. Place on work surface. Set oven temperature at 450°F.
• Cut each mushroom crosswise into ½-inch-wide strips. Alternate mushroom strips and cheese strips atop each bread slice. Place bread on baking sheet. Bake until cheese melts, about 5 minutes.
• *6 servings*

Melted Cheese Dip with Tortilla Chips

For this dip, based on the Mexican *queso fundido*, you will need to use a flameproof dish set over candles or Sterno to keep the cheese melted. Blue corn tortilla chips add a shot of color. This is a natural with the South-of-the-Border Party (page 84).

1 pound Monterey Jack cheese, grated
2 tablespoons all purpose flour
1/2 cup plus 2 tablespoons beer
1/4 cup chopped fresh cilantro
2 teaspoons minced jalapeño chilies
Blue corn tortilla chips

• Place cheese in large bowl. Add flour and toss to coat. Bring beer to boil in heavy large saucepan. Reduce heat to low. Add 1 handful of cheese to beer; stir constantly until cheese melts. Repeat with remaining cheese; stir until thick and creamy (do not boil). Stir in cilantro and chilies. Season with salt and pepper. Pour into flameproof baking dish.
• If desired, preheat broiler. Broil cheese dip until top is golden, about 2 minutes. Set dish over candles or Sterno on serving table. Serve with tortilla chips.
• *6 servings*

Roasted Portobello Mushrooms with Fontina (far left); Melted Cheese Dip with Tortilla Chips (left)

Red Bell Pepper Dip

This delicious dip, which can be made a day ahead, would be a welcome starter at any number of menus, from the Picnic in the Country (page 48) to The Brunch on page 112.

1   small red onion, quartered
1   teaspoon olive oil

1   7-ounce jar roasted red bell peppers, drained
12   fresh basil leaves or 1/2 teaspoon dried
12   ounces cream cheese, room temperature

  Bagel chips
  Chilled blanched asparagus
  Cherry tomatoes
  Red, green and/or yellow bell pepper strips
  Mushrooms

• Preheat oven to 400°F. Place onion in small baking dish. Drizzle oil over. Bake until soft, about 45 minutes. Cool.
• Puree onion with roasted bell peppers and basil leaves in processor. Add cream cheese and blend just until combined. Transfer to medium bowl. Cover and refrigerate dip at least 3 hours. *(Can be prepared 1 day ahead.)*
• Place dip in center of platter. Surround dip with bagel chips, blanched asparagus, cherry tomatoes, bell pepper strips and mushrooms.
• *Makes about 2 ½ cups*

Avocado and Mozzarella with Vinaigrette

This simple starter of chunks of avocado and mozzarella tossed with a vinaigrette would make a fine addition to the Pizza Party menu (page 70), replacing the salsa and garlic toasts.

1/2   cup olive oil
3   tablespoons red wine vinegar
1   garlic clove, minced
3   ripe avocados, halved, pitted, peeled, cubed
15   ounces (about) fresh mozzarella in water,* drained, cubed
1/4   cup chopped fresh basil

• Whisk first 3 ingredients in large bowl to blend. Add avocados, mozzarella and basil and toss. Season with salt and pepper.
* *Fresh mozzarella is available at specialty foods stores and some supermarkets.*
• *6 servings*

Four-Pepper Salsa with Chips

An easy starter that could stand in for the Picadillo and Pico de Gallo in the South-of-the-Border Party (page 84).

1   14 1/2-ounce can Italian plum tomatoes, drained
1   medium onion, thinly sliced
1/2   cup coarsely chopped celery
1   4-ounce can diced green chilies, drained
1/3   cup chopped red bell pepper
1/3   cup chopped yellow bell pepper
1/3   cup chopped green bell pepper
1/4   cup olive oil
2   tablespoons red wine vinegar
1   teaspoon mustard seeds
1   teaspoon ground coriander
1   teaspoon salt
1   teaspoon pepper
1/4   cup chopped fresh cilantro
  Tortilla chips

• Combine first 13 ingredients in processor. Finely chop using on/off turns. Transfer to bowl. Cover and chill at least 4 hours. *(Can be made 2 days ahead.)* Mix cilantro into salsa. Serve with chips.
• *Makes about 3 ½ cups*

Blue Cheese Bread

A quick and savory starter or accompaniment to everything from the roast beef in The Potluck menu on page 126, to the pasta main courses in the Pasta Party (page 34; halve the recipe).

8   ounces blue cheese
1   cup (2 sticks) unsalted butter, room temperature

2   French bread baguettes or 4 sourdough flutes (2 pounds total), halved lengthwise
  Chopped celery tops

• Blend cheese and butter in processor until smooth. *(Can be prepared 2 days ahead. Cover and refrigerate. Bring cheese mixture to room temperature before using.)*
• Preheat broiler. Broil bread crust side up until crisp. Turn and broil cut side until light brown. Spread cheese mixture over cut side of bread. Sprinkle liberally with pepper. Broil until cheese bubbles and begins to brown. Remove from broiler and sprinkle bread with celery. Cut crosswise into 1-inch pieces.
• *12 servings*

Pesto Torte

This delicious appetizer comprises layers of pesto, cream cheese and ricotta mixed together, and pine nuts, all molded in a bowl and then turned out for an impressive presentation. You could easily take it along for the Picnic in the Country (page 48). (The leftover pesto can be frozen up to one month. Place it in a freezer container and cover with a thin layer of olive oil.)

PESTO

1	garlic clove
1 1/2	cups (packed) fresh basil leaves
1/2	cup pine nuts (about 21/2 ounces)
1/2	cup freshly grated Parmesan cheese
1/3	cup olive oil

TORTE

1 1/2	8-ounce packages cream cheese, room temperature
3/4	cup ricotta cheese, room temperature
3/4	cup (1 1/2 sticks) butter, room temperature
5	tablespoons pine nuts

Assorted breads and crackers

• FOR PESTO: Drop garlic through feed tube of processor and process until minced. Add basil, pine nuts and cheese; process until minced. Gradually add oil and process to coarse puree. Season to taste with salt and pepper.

• FOR TORTE: Blend cream cheese, ricotta cheese and butter in processor until smooth. Line deep 6-cup bowl with plastic wrap. Sprinkle 1 tablespoon pine nuts in bottom of bowl. Spoon ⅓ of cheese mixture into bowl; smooth top. Spread half of pesto over cheese (save remaining pesto for another use). Sprinkle with 2 tablespoons pine nuts. Spoon half of remaining cheese mixture over pine nuts; smooth top. Sprinkle with 2 tablespoons pine nuts. Spoon remaining cheese mixture over pine nuts. Cover top with plastic wrap; refrigerate until firm, about 4 hours. *(Can be made 1 day ahead. Keep refrigerated.)*

• Uncover torte and unmold onto serving platter. Bring to room temperature. Serve with breads and crackers.

• *8 servings*

Black-eyed Pea Dip (right);
Caviar Pie (far right)

Black-eyed Pea Dip

This new variation on the classic bean dip would make a good starter for the South-of-the-Border Party (page 84).

1 1/4 cups dried black-eyed peas
   2 garlic cloves, sliced

   1 3-ounce package cream cheese, room temperature
   1 teaspoon cayenne pepper
   1 teaspoon chili powder

1 1/2 cups shredded cheddar cheese (about 6 ounces)
   1 bunch green onions, sliced
      Tortilla chips

• Place peas in heavy medium saucepan. Add enough water to saucepan to cover peas by 2 inches. Let stand 30 minutes. Drain. Add water to cover peas by 2 inches. Generously salt water. Stir in 1 garlic clove. Boil until peas are very tender, adding more water to pan if necessary, about 1 hour.
• Using slotted spoon, transfer peas to processor. Process until smooth. Add remaining garlic clove and next 3 ingredients. Pulse until smooth. Season to taste with salt and pepper. Transfer dip to 8-inch-diameter pie plate or quiche dish. (*Can be prepared 2 days ahead. Cover and refrigerate.*)
• Preheat oven to 400°F. Top dip with cheddar. Bake until dip is heated through and cheese bubbles, about 20 minutes. Sprinkle dip with green onions and serve with tortilla chips.
• *6 servings*

Baked Brie with Caramelized Onions

Reminiscent of fondue, this rich appetizer would fit in nicely with the other dishes in the Bistro Supper (page 42). (You may need to order the uncut wheel of cheese from a cheese shop or specialty foods store.)

   2 tablespoons (1/4 stick) butter
   8 cups sliced onions (about 4 large)
   1 tablespoon minced fresh thyme
   4 garlic cloves, chopped
 1/2 cup dry white wine
   1 teaspoon sugar

   1 8-inch-diameter 32- to 36-ounce French Brie, packed in wooden box (reserve box)
   2 French bread baguettes, sliced

• Melt butter in heavy very large skillet over medium-high heat. Add onions; sauté until just tender, about 6 minutes. Add minced thyme, reduce heat to medium and cook until onions are golden, stirring often, about 25 minutes. Add garlic and sauté 2 minutes. Add ¼ cup wine; stir until almost all liquid evaporates, about 2 minutes. Sprinkle sugar over onions and sauté until soft and brown, about 10 minutes. Add remaining ¼ cup wine; stir just until liquid evaporates, about 2 minutes. Season to taste with salt and pepper. Cool. (*Can be prepared 2 days ahead. Cover onion mixture and refrigerate.*)
• Preheat oven to 350°F. Unwrap Brie, reserving bottom of wooden box. Cut away only top rind of cheese, leaving rind on sides and bottom intact. Return Brie to box, rind side down. Place box on baking sheet. Top Brie evenly with onion mixture. Bake until cheese just melts, about 30 minutes. Transfer Brie in box to platter. Surround with baguette slices.
• *8 to 10 servings*

Caviar Pie

The impressive look of this layered spread belies its simplicity. Add it to the Cocktails at Five menu (page 18).

      Nonstick vegetable oil spray
   1 small onion, finely chopped
 1/2 teaspoon sugar
 10 hard-boiled eggs, peeled
 1/4 cup low-fat mayonnaise
   2 tablespoons sweet pickle relish

   1 8-ounce "brick" Neufchâtel cheese (reduced-fat cream cheese), room temperature
   1 tablespoon milk

   8 ounces caviar (preferably 2 or more colors)
      Lemon slices
      Chopped parsley
      Assorted crackers

• Spray 9-inch-diameter tart pan with removable bottom or 9-inch-diameter springform pan with vegetable oil spray. Combine onion and sugar in medium bowl. Place 10 egg whites and 6 yolks in processor (reserve remaining yolks for another use). Chop coarsely. Add mayonnaise and relish and process just until combined (do not overmix to paste). Add to bowl with onion and blend well. Spread over bottom of prepared pan. Refrigerate 15 minutes.
• Combine Neufchâtel cheese and milk in processor. Blend well. Drop cheese mixture by teaspoonfuls over chilled egg layer and spread gently to cover. Refrigerate until firm, about 1 hour. (*Can be prepared 1 day ahead. Cover with plastic and keep refrigerated.*)
• Spoon caviar decoratively atop cheese layer. Garnish with lemon slices and parsley. Press bottom of tart pan up or remove sides of springform pan, releasing pie. Place pie on platter; surround with crackers.
• *16 servings*

the brunch

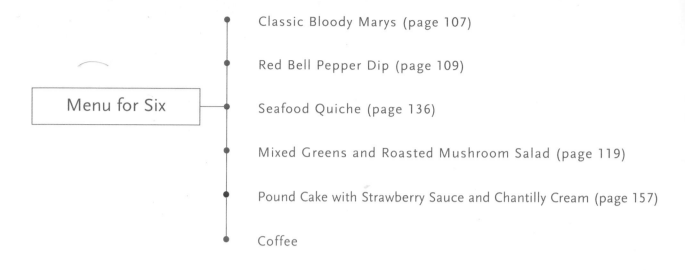

- Classic Bloody Marys (page 107)

- Red Bell Pepper Dip (page 109)

Menu for Six

- Seafood Quiche (page 136)

- Mixed Greens and Roasted Mushroom Salad (page 119)

- Pound Cake with Strawberry Sauce and Chantilly Cream (page 157)

- Coffee

When you're stirring a tall Bloody Mary in the middle of the day and leaning back in your deck chair to catch the sun, you can appreciate fully the allure of brunch: It is a wonderful way to while away a few hours, an instant reprieve from the ought-to's and should-do's that otherwise gobble up free time. ★ Brunch is also the most flexible meal to schedule and serve. It can top off a round of golf or a tennis game. Or it can announce a festive occasion, whether Mother's Day or a graduation. It comes well ahead of Sunday night's dash to prepare for school or work. And, if there are children coming, parents will tell you it's their best time of day. ★ The balance of food is important — not too heavy but satisfying enough to make the single meal stand in for two. The balance of preparations is critical — no cook should have to wake up early to face long hours in the kitchen before guests arrive. This menu gets it all just right: The luxury of a seafood quiche with the crisp counterpoint of an easy but change-of-pace greens and roasted mushroom salad, and a dessert of purchased pound cake with strawberries and whipped cream. The Bloody Marys, with their vegetable "bundle" stirrers, the intriguing but simple red pepper dip, the quiche crust, the roasted mushrooms and the dessert sauce can all be done a day ahead. ★ So if you take a few minutes to set the table the night before, you can enjoy the best of two worlds in the morning: a little extra time in bed and a brunch worth getting up for.

mix-and-match soups, salads and sides

soups

Potato-Leek Soup

If you're looking to start the Pasta Party (page 34) off with something warm and comforting, try this satisfying soup in place of the antipasto platter and mushrooms and peppers dish. Its creamy texture belies the fact that it contains no cream at all.

- 2 tablespoons olive oil
- 2 leeks (white and pale green parts only), chopped
- 3 cups canned low-salt chicken broth
- 2 pounds celery root (about 2), peeled, cut into 1/4-inch-thick slices
- 1 pound russet potatoes (about 2), peeled, cut into 1-inch pieces

- 2 cups (about) milk

- 1/4 cup minced fresh parsley
- 3 tablespoons minced red onion
- 2 teaspoons grated orange peel

• Heat oil in heavy large saucepan over medium-low heat. Add leeks and sauté until tender, about 10 minutes. Add chicken broth, celery root and potatoes. Cover and simmer until vegetables are very tender, about 45 minutes.
• Puree broth mixture in batches in blender or processor until smooth. Return mixture to saucepan. Add enough milk to thin soup to desired consistency. Season to taste with salt and pepper. *(Can be prepared up to 1 day ahead. Cover and refrigerate.)*
• Combine parsley, onion and orange peel in small bowl. Bring soup to simmer. Ladle into bowls. Sprinkle with parsley mixture and serve.
• *6 servings*

Spring Greens Soup

This light and colorful soup would work well in the Lunch on the Terrace menu (page 28). If you're short on time, use canned chicken broth in place of the homemade stock.

    1   pound chicken necks, backs
        and/or wings, fat removed, rinsed
    7   cups cold water
    4   slices fresh ginger
    2   green onions
    2   garlic cloves, lightly crushed
        with side of large knife

    5   dried shiitake mushrooms

    2   cups trimmed, chopped beet
        greens, dandelion greens or
        Swiss chard
  1/4   cup thinly sliced carrot
    1   tablespoon matchstick-size
        strips peeled fresh ginger
   12   sugar snap peas
  1/2   cup diced firm tofu
    1   green onion, sliced

• Bring first 5 ingredients to boil in heavy large saucepan. Skim off any foam from top with slotted spoon. Reduce heat to low. Simmer chicken stock until liquid is reduced to 6 cups, about 1½ hours. Strain stock and refrigerate overnight. *(Can be prepared 2 days ahead.)*
• Place shiitake mushrooms in small bowl. Cover mushrooms with hot water. Let stand until mushrooms are soft, about 15 minutes. Drain. Slice caps into matchstick-size strips, discarding stems.
• Remove any fat from surface of stock. Bring stock to simmer. Add chopped greens, carrot and ginger strips. Simmer until carrots are just tender, about 8 minutes. Add shiitake mushrooms and sugar snap peas and continue cooking until peas are crisp-tender, about 3 minutes. Stir in tofu and sliced green onion. Season with salt and serve.

• *4 servings*

Classic Gazpacho

Gazpacho is a good dinner party soup since it can be prepared ahead and refrigerated, making the evening's first course one less thing to do. Try this fresh-tasting version in place of the other appetizers in the South-of-the-Border Party (page 84).

    2   large tomatoes (about 1 pound)
    1   large cucumber, peeled, halved
        lengthwise, seeded
    1   medium onion
    1   large roasted red bell pepper
    3   cups tomato juice
  1/2   cup chopped fresh cilantro
  1/3   cup red wine vinegar
  1/4   cup olive oil
  1/8   teaspoon hot pepper sauce
        (such as Tabasco)

• Cut 1 tomato, ½ cucumber and ½ onion into 1-inch pieces and transfer to processor. Add bell pepper and puree. Transfer to bowl. Add tomato juice, cilantro, vinegar, oil and hot pepper sauce. Seed remaining tomato. Dice remaining tomato and cucumber and onion halves and add to soup. Season with salt and pepper. Refrigerate. *(Can be prepared 2 days ahead.)* Serve well chilled.
• *6 servings*

Classic Gazpacho

Chilled Tomato and Orange Soup

This lovely, refreshing soup would make an excellent beginning to the Dinner and a Movie menu (page 78). Make it up to two days ahead, and serve it in place of the stuffed mushrooms.

    6   medium oranges

    3   tablespoons unsalted butter
  1 1/2 cups thinly sliced yellow onions
  1/2   cup thinly sliced fennel bulb
  2 1/2 pounds plum tomatoes,
        quartered
  1/2   cup dry white wine
    1   tablespoon grated orange peel
    1   bay leaf
    1   teaspoon salt
  3 1/2 cups canned low-salt
        chicken broth

  1/2   cup sour cream or plain yogurt
        Fresh basil sprigs

• Using small sharp knife, cut off peel and white pith from oranges. Working over bowl to catch juice, cut between membranes to release segments.
• Melt butter in heavy large saucepan over low heat. Add sliced onions and fennel and sauté 10 minutes. Add half of oranges with their juices and half of tomatoes and simmer 10 minutes, stirring occasionally. Add dry white wine, grated orange peel, bay leaf and salt. Mix in remaining oranges with their juices, remaining tomatoes and chicken broth. Bring to boil. Reduce heat to medium and cook soup 10 minutes, stirring occasionally. Discard bay leaf.
• Puree soup in blender or processor in batches. Cover and chill soup until cold. *(Can be prepared 2 days ahead.)*
• Ladle soup into bowls. Top with dollops of sour cream. Garnish with fresh basil sprigs and serve.

• *6 to 8 servings*

Minted Cucumber Buttermilk Soup

Another "summery" soup, this creamy chilled one could replace the Yellow Bell Pepper Soup in the Lunch on the Terrace (page 28).

1 1/2   pounds English hothouse cucumbers, peeled, quartered, seeded
    2   cups buttermilk
  1/4   cup chopped onion
    2   garlic cloves
    1   cup sour cream
    1   cup plain low-fat yogurt
    2   tablespoons chopped fresh mint
    1   tablespoon chopped fresh chives or green onion tops
    1   tablespoon fresh lemon juice
    2   teaspoons sugar
        Pinch of cayenne pepper

        Fresh mint sprigs

• Puree cucumbers, buttermilk, chopped onion and garlic in blender until smooth. Transfer to bowl. Stir in sour cream, yogurt, chopped mint, chives, lemon juice, sugar and cayenne. Season to taste with salt and pepper. Cover and refrigerate until well chilled. *(Can be prepared 1 day ahead.)*
• Stir soup. Ladle into bowls. Garnish soup with mint sprigs.
• *4 to 6 servings*

salads

Sweet-and-Sour Coleslaw

Try this unusual slaw in place of the potato salad in the Back-Yard Barbecue (page 56). (If you like your coleslaw crunchy, serve it within two hours of preparation. If you like it softer, chill six hours or overnight.)

  1/3   cup cider vinegar
  1/4   cup apple juice or apple cider
    2   tablespoons vegetable oil
    1   garlic clove, minced
    1   teaspoon sugar
  1/2   teaspoon salt
    4   cups finely shredded red cabbage (about 1/2 small head)
    4   cups finely shredded green cabbage (about 1/2 small head)
    1   large carrot, coarsely shredded
  1/4   cup finely chopped fresh parsley

• Whisk cider vinegar, apple juice, vegetable oil, minced garlic, sugar and salt in large bowl to blend. Add remaining ingredients and toss well to mix. Season with pepper. Cover and refrigerate until cold, tossing occasionally, about 2 hours.
• *6 servings*

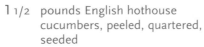

Minted Cucumber Buttermilk Soup (above); Sweet-and-Sour Coleslaw (right); Warm Orange and Mushroom Spinach Salad (far right)

Warm Orange and Mushroom Spinach Salad

For a different kind of salad, try this one in place of the Portobello Mushrooms and Roasted Peppers with Soy-Balsamic Vinaigrette in the Pasta Party menu (page 34).

DRESSING

8 ounces sliced bacon, cut into 1-inch pieces
3/4 cup orange juice
1/4 cup plus 2 tablespoons minced shallots
1/4 cup olive oil
1/4 cup balsamic vinegar

SALAD

4 oranges, peeled, white pith removed
10 ounces spinach, stems trimmed
1 medium head radicchio

6 ounces fresh shiitake mushrooms, stemmed, sliced
6 ounces fresh oyster mushrooms
1/2 cup (generous) toasted hazelnuts, coarsely chopped
1 3 1/2-ounce package enoki mushrooms (optional)

• FOR DRESSING: Cook bacon in heavy large skillet over medium heat until crisp. Using slotted spoon, transfer bacon to paper towels. Pour off drippings and reserve. Combine ¼ cup reserved drippings with remaining ingredients in small bowl. Season to taste with salt and pepper.

• FOR SALAD: Working over small bowl and using small sharp knife, cut between membranes of oranges to release segments; add to bowl. Tear spinach and radicchio into bite-size pieces and place in large bowl. (Can be prepared 1 day ahead. Cover dressing, orange segments, greens and reserved bacon drippings separately and refrigerate.)

• Drain orange segments. Heat 2 tablespoons reserved bacon drippings in heavy large skillet over medium-high heat. Add sliced shiitake mushrooms and sauté 1 minute. Add oyster mushrooms and season with salt and pepper. Sauté until golden brown, about 2 minutes. Add mushrooms to greens and toss. Pour dressing into same skillet and boil 2 minutes. Pour dressing over greens. Add bacon, orange segments and chopped hazelnuts. Toss to combine. Season to taste with salt and pepper. Garnish salad with enoki mushrooms.

• 4 to 6 servings

Green Bean and Tomato Salad

This colorful, quick-to-prepare salad makes an appearance in The Potluck menu on page 126; you might also try it in the Dinner and a Movie menu (halve the recipe) on page 78.

3 pounds green beans, trimmed, cut into 2-inch pieces
3 tablespoons country-style Dijon mustard
1/4 cup Sherry wine vinegar
2/3 cup olive oil
1/3 cup minced shallots
2 1-pint baskets cherry tomatoes, halved

• Cook beans in large pot of boiling salted water until crisp-tender, about 5 minutes. Drain. Refresh under cold water; drain well. Transfer to large bowl. Combine mustard and vinegar in small bowl. Gradually whisk in oil. Mix in shallots. (Can be prepared 1 day ahead. Cover beans and dressing separately. Refrigerate beans; let dressing stand at room temperature.) Mix dressing and tomatoes into beans. Season to taste with salt and pepper.

• 12 servings

Potato, Roasted Pepper and Arugula Salad

Potato salad—but different. This delicious do-ahead version turns up in The Potluck menu on page 126. It would also work (halve the recipe) in the Back-Yard Barbecue menu on page 56.

7 pounds red potatoes, cut into 3/4-inch pieces
2/3 cup dry white wine

4 red bell peppers
2 yellow bell peppers

2 1 3/4- to 2-ounce cans flat fillets of anchovies, drained, minced
1/4 cup plus 2 tablespoons white wine vinegar
1 1/2 cups olive oil
2 green onion bunches, sliced
2 fresh arugula bunches, sliced

• Place potatoes in large pot. Cover with water. Boil until potatoes are just tender. Drain well. Transfer to large bowl. Mix in white wine.

• Char peppers over gas flame or in broiler until blackened on all sides. Wrap in paper bag and let stand 10 minutes. Peel and seed. Rinse if necessary; pat dry. Cut peppers into ¾-inch squares. Transfer to medium bowl.

• Combine anchovies and vinegar in small bowl. Gradually whisk in oil. Pour ⅔ cup dressing over peppers. Add remaining dressing, green onions and arugula to potatoes and mix gently. Season peppers and potatoes with salt and pepper. Let stand 30 minutes. Gently mix peppers into potatoes. (Can be prepared 1 day ahead. Cover and refrigerate. Bring to room temperature before serving.)

• 12 servings

Tomatoes with Fresh Herbs and Spiced Vinaigrette

If you can get green and yellow tomatoes in addition to the usual red, they add vibrant color to this refreshing side dish; but the dish is just as nice when made with only red tomatoes. You could serve this instead of one of the other salads in the Picnic in the Country menu (page 48).

> 3 tablespoons balsamic vinegar
> 2 tablespoons fresh lime juice
> 1 tablespoon Hungarian sweet paprika
> 1 teaspoon curry powder
> 1/2 teaspoon chili powder
> 1/2 cup olive oil
>
> 2 1/2 pounds tomatoes, sliced into 1/3-inch-thick rounds
> 2 tablespoons chopped chives or green onions (optional)
> Fresh basil leaves
> Fresh cilantro leaves

• Combine first 5 ingredients in small bowl. Gradually whisk in oil. Season dressing with salt and pepper. *(Can be made 1 day ahead. Cover tightly.)*
• Overlap tomatoes on platter. Spoon dressing over. Top with chives, if desired. Garnish with basil and cilantro leaves.
• *8 servings*

Eggplant, Squash and Tomato with Roasted Garlic Vinaigrette

A colorful option to the Mixed Greens and Fennel Salad in the Pizza Party menu (page 70).

> 4 large garlic cloves, unpeeled
> Olive oil
> 1 1/2 tablespoons balsamic vinegar
> 1/3 cup olive oil
>
> 3 large Japanese eggplants, cut crosswise into 1/2-inch-thick rounds
> 3 large yellow summer squash or zucchini, cut crosswise into 1/2-inch-thick rounds
>
> 3 tomatoes, thinly sliced
> 16 fresh basil leaves, chopped

• Preheat oven to 350°F. Place unpeeled garlic cloves in small baking dish. Drizzle garlic with olive oil and toss to coat. Roast garlic until very tender, about 25 minutes. Cool. Peel garlic and mince. Transfer to small bowl. Mix in balsamic vinegar. Gradually mix in ⅓ cup olive oil.
• Preheat broiler. Arrange eggplant slices in single layer on broiler pan. Brush both sides with olive oil. Sprinkle with salt and pepper. Broil until beginning to brown, about 4 minutes per side. Arrange squash slices in single layer on broiler pan. Brush tops of squash with olive oil; season with salt and pepper. Broil until tops begin to brown, about 4 minutes.
• Alternate eggplant and squash slices around edge of serving platter, overlapping slightly. Arrange tomato slices in center of platter. Sprinkle tomatoes with salt and pepper. Drizzle dressing over salad. *(Salad can be prepared 2 hours ahead. Cover and let stand at room temperature.)* Sprinkle salad with chopped fresh basil and serve.
• *6 servings*

Tomatoes with Fresh Herbs and Spiced Vinaigrette (below left); Eggplant, Squash and Tomato with Roasted Garlic Vinaigrette (below right)

Prosciutto, Pear and Fennel Salad

This sophisticated and easy-to-make starter might replace the crudités in the Lunch on the Terrace menu (page 28).

1	large Bartlett or Anjou pear, peeled, cored, cut into 1/2-inch pieces
2	tablespoons Sherry wine vinegar
1/2	cup coarsely chopped fresh fennel bulb
1/3	cup chopped walnuts, toasted
1/4	cup olive oil
1	tablespoon minced fennel fronds
8	thin prosciutto slices

•Combine pear and vinegar in medium bowl. Add fennel bulb, walnuts, oil and fennel fronds. Season with salt and pepper and toss to blend.
• Cross 2 prosciutto slices on each of 4 plates, forming an X. Spoon pear mixture onto center of prosciutto slices, dividing equally. Serve.

• *4 servings*

Mixed Greens and Roasted Mushroom Salad

This attractive salad, which gets served with the quiche in The Brunch menu on page 112, would make a nice addition to virtually any menu, including the Garden Party on page 92.

5	tablespoons balsamic vinegar
1	tablespoon Dijon mustard
1/2	teaspoon dried thyme
2/3	cup olive oil
3/4	pound mushrooms, quartered
1	head radicchio, leaves torn into bite-size pieces
2	heads Belgian endive, cut crosswise into 1-inch-wide pieces
1	head curly endive (inner leaves only), torn into bite-size pieces
1/2	small red onion, thinly sliced
1/2	fresh chive bunch, cut into 1-inch-long pieces

• Preheat oven to 400°F. Whisk first 3 ingredients in small bowl. Gradually whisk in oil. Season to taste with salt and pepper. *(Can be prepared 1 day ahead. Cover and store at room temperature.)* Place mushrooms on baking sheet. Pour ¼ cup dressing over and toss to coat. Bake until mushrooms are crisp on edges, about 15 minutes. Cool.
• Combine mushrooms, radicchio, Belgian endive, curly endive, sliced red onion and chives in large bowl. Add enough remaining dressing to season to taste and toss well. Divide salad among plates and serve immediately.

• *8 servings*

Flower Power

There are few easier ways to give a table style than with flowers. They can set the tone, be it casual or elegant, spark the setting and scent the scene. And while we've all had to resort to that grocery-store bouquet on occasion, a little imagination in the way of flowers, arrangement and vases can go a long way. Here are some ideas.

An old-fashioned bouquet of lilacs, daffodils or daisies in an antique milk bottle or pitcher, large canning jar or garden watering can.

A small bunch of garden roses clustered in a teapot.

Boughs of forsythia, dogwood or apple blossoms anchored in a tall pottery canister, wooden bucket (with a jar of water inside) or even a large ice bucket.

Small pots of cacti, herbs or grape hyacinths grouped in a low, flat-bottomed basket, such as a bamboo steamer basket, or on a rimmed tray. Fill in the spaces around the pots with shells or pebbles.

A big bunch of dried hydrangea, statice, silver dollars, cattails or even autumn leaves in a straw waste basket, fire-wood holder or antique umbrella stand.

A large pot of geraniums or tulips tied with a scarf or napkin. Or, arrange several smaller pots in a deep, handled basket, a wooden flower box or an antique ceramic or copper basin.

Tomato Salad with Basil-Buttermilk Dressing

This salad gets The Cookout on page 148 off to a delicious start, but it would also be a nice addition to the Picnic in the Country menu (page 48).

2	cups packed fresh basil leaves (about 2 large bunches)
3/4	cup buttermilk
2	green onions, thinly sliced
3/4	teaspoon salt
3/4	cup mayonnaise
1/2	teaspoon pepper
4	pounds firm ripe tomatoes
	Fresh basil sprigs

• Blend 2 cups fresh basil, buttermilk, sliced green onions and salt in processor until smooth. Transfer to bowl. Add mayonnaise and pepper and whisk until dressing is smooth. Let stand 30 minutes. Season to taste with salt and pepper. *(Can be made 8 hours ahead. Cover tightly and refrigerate.)*
• Core and slice tomatoes. Arrange on platter. Spoon enough dressing over tomatoes to coat. Garnish with basil sprigs. Serve, passing extra dressing separately.
• *8 servings*

Salad Bowl Pasta

side dishes

Potato Gratin with Boursin

A sinfully rich and delicious side dish, perfect in the Bistro Supper (page 42), standing in for the galette.

2	cups whipping cream
1	5-ounce package Boursin cheese with herbs
3	pounds red new potatoes (unpeeled), scrubbed, thinly sliced
1 1/2	tablespoons chopped fresh parsley

• Preheat oven to 400°F. Butter 9 x 13-inch baking dish with 2-inch-high sides. Stir whipping cream and Boursin cheese in heavy large saucepan over medium heat until cheese melts and mixture is smooth. Arrange half of sliced potatoes in baking dish in slightly overlapping rows. Generously season potatoes in dish with salt and pepper. Pour half of cheese mixture over. Arrange remaining potatoes in slightly overlapping rows atop potatoes in dish. Generously season with salt and pepper. Pour remaining cheese mixture over potatoes. Bake until top is golden brown and potatoes are tender when pierced with knife, about 1 hour. Sprinkle with chopped fresh parsley and serve.
• *8 servings*

Salad Bowl Pasta

This quick and colorful pasta dish would go well with the scampi in the Dinner and a Movie menu (page 78), replacing the Caesar salad.

1 1/2	1-pint baskets cherry tomatoes, halved
1 1/2	1-pint baskets yellow pear tomatoes or cherry tomatoes, halved
4	tablespoons olive oil
1	medium red onion, finely chopped
1	ear fresh corn, kernels removed
6	green onions, thinly sliced on diagonal, white and green parts separated
2	large garlic cloves, minced
12	ounces tiny pasta shells
5	ounces ricotta salata or mild feta cheese, cut into small dice
1/4	cup finely shredded fresh basil
2/3	cup freshly grated Parmesan cheese
	Additional grated Parmesan cheese

• Place tomatoes in nonaluminum colander. Sprinkle lightly with salt; let tomatoes drain 30 minutes.
• Heat 3 tablespoons oil in heavy large skillet over medium heat. Add red onion, corn kernels, white parts of green onions and garlic. Sauté until onions just begin to wilt, about 7 minutes.
• Cook pasta in large pot of boiling salted water until just tender but still firm to bite. Drain, reserving 1 cup cooking liquid. Return pasta to same pot. Add onion mixture, tomatoes, green part of onions, ricotta salata, basil, ½ cup grated Parmesan cheese, remaining 1 tablespoon olive oil and ¼ cup reserved cooking liquid. Toss over medium heat until heated through, adding more reserved cooking liquid and Parmesan cheese as needed to form light sauce. Season with salt and pepper. Serve, passing additional Parmesan separately.
• *6 servings*

Herbed Potatoes

These tasty grilled potatoes could stand in for the focaccia in the Garden Party menu (page 92).

3	pounds small red potatoes, unpeeled
6	tablespoons malt vinegar
5	tablespoons olive oil
1 1/2	tablespoons dried oregano
1 1/2	tablespoons minced fresh thyme or 1/4 teaspoon dried
1	tablespoon pepper
3/4	teaspoon salt

• Place potatoes in large pot and cover with cold water. Boil until almost tender, about 30 minutes. Drain and cool. Cut crosswise into ½-inch-thick rounds.
• Whisk remaining ingredients in large bowl to blend. Add potatoes and toss thoroughly to coat. Cover and let stand 1 hour at room temperature.
• Prepare barbecue (medium heat). Remove potatoes from marinade and place on grill; reserve marinade. Cook potatoes until golden brown, turning occasionally, about 12 minutes. Transfer to platter. Brush remaining marinade over and then serve.

• *8 servings*

Three-Onion Sauté

An easy and deliciously different side dish that might replace the couscous in Dinner in the Kitchen (page 10).

1/4	cup olive oil
2	leeks, halved, sliced
2	medium red onions, halved, sliced
1	medium onion, halved, sliced
1/2	cup canned chicken broth
3	tablespoons Sherry vinegar
2	tablespoons sugar
1/8	teaspoon ground cloves

• Heat oil in heavy large skillet over medium heat. Add leeks and onions. Cover and cook 10 minutes. Uncover and cook until tender, stirring occasionally, about 30 minutes. Add broth, vinegar, sugar and cloves. Simmer until liquid is syrupy, stirring constantly, about 7 minutes. Season with salt and pepper. Serve warm or at room temperature.
• *6 servings*

Rice Pilaf with Peas and Pine Nuts

To fill out the Lunch on the Terrace menu (page 28), cook up this quick rice side dish.

2	tablespoons (1/4 stick) butter
1	onion, finely chopped
1 1/2	cups long-grain white rice
1	teaspoon ground turmeric
4	cups canned chicken broth
1	cup frozen peas
1/2	cup toasted pine nuts

• Melt butter in heavy large saucepan over medium heat. Add chopped onion and sauté until tender, about 5 minutes. Add rice and turmeric and stir 1 minute. Mix in broth. Cover and simmer over low heat until rice is almost tender, about 15 minutes. Add peas, cover and continue simmering until rice is tender and liquid is absorbed, about 5 minutes. Season with salt and pepper. Transfer to bowl and sprinkle with toasted pine nuts.
• *4 servings*

Grilled Red Onions

Simply great, these grilled onion rings accompany hamburgers in The Cookout on page 148. Or stick them on the grill with the corn in the Garden Party menu (page 92).

4	medium red onions
2	tablespoons Worcestershire sauce
2	tablespoons balsamic vinegar
2	tablespoons soy sauce
2	tablespoons olive oil
3/4	teaspoon pepper

• Cut ¼-inch slice off top and bottom of each onion and discard. Cut onions in half crosswise. Arrange onions in single layer in shallow dish. Whisk Worcestershire, vinegar, soy sauce and oil in bowl. Pour over onions and let stand at room temperature 1 hour, basting occasionally.
• Prepare barbecue (medium-high heat). Arrange onions on grill. Cover grill and cook onions until brown, basting occasionally, about 4 minutes per side. Using large spatula, transfer onions to platter. Season with pepper.
• *8 servings*

The Newer Napkin

A napkin needn't be a napkin; it can also be a dish towel (especially useful at a picnic), a finger towel (linen, terry cloth or paper), a bandana or, if the food is sparerib-type saucy, a moistened washcloth. And a napkin needn't be folded into the predictable triangle or rectangle; instead, it can be arranged like this:

Knotted in the middle and laid across the plate.

Draped, by grasping it in the middle and laying it on the plate.

Rolled up and tied with ribbon, gold cord or, if you're feeling playful, licorice strings.

Pulled through wooden bangle bracelets, or, for brunch, bagels.

Wrapped like cones around buffet flatware and arranged on a tray or in a basket.

Tied around a single flower, a few sprigs of rosemary and thyme or a long dinner roll.

Hot and Smoky Baked Beans

This delicious version of the classic is made with white beans, and accompanies burgers and ribs in The Cookout menu on page 148. But there isn't an outdoor meal this dish wouldn't be welcome at, including the Garden Party on page 92.

3 1/2	cups (about 1 pound 7 ounces) dried Great Northern white beans, picked over
1	smoked ham hock (about 4 ounces)
3 1/2	teaspoons salt
2	cups finely chopped onion
1 1/4	cups purchased barbecue sauce
1	12-ounce jar hot salsa
1/3	cup firmly packed golden brown sugar
1/4	cup Dijon mustard
1/4	cup light unsulfured molasses

• Place white beans in heavy large Dutch oven. Cover beans generously with cold water. Bring to boil over medium-high heat. Remove from heat and let stand until cool, about 1 hour.
• Drain white beans. Return to same pot. Cover beans generously with cold water. Add smoked ham hock to pot and bring to boil over medium-high heat. Reduce heat to low and simmer bean mixture 20 minutes. Add 2 teaspoons salt and simmer until beans are tender, stirring occasionally, about 20 minutes longer. Remove ham hock and reserve. Drain white beans, reserving 1½ cups bean cooking liquid.
• Position rack in center of oven and preheat to 350°F. Combine cooked beans, reserved 1½ cups bean cooking liquid, finely chopped onion, barbecue sauce, hot salsa, golden brown sugar, Dijon mustard, light molasses and remaining 1½ teaspoons salt in same large pot. Push reserved ham hock into center of bean mixture.

• Cover pot and bake bean mixture 1 hour. Uncover and bake until bean mixture is very thick, stirring occasionally, about 40 minutes longer. *(Beans can be prepared 1 day ahead. Cover tightly and refrigerate. Before serving, rewarm over low heat, stirring frequently.)* Remove ham hock and discard. Transfer beans to large bowl and serve.
• *8 servings*

Minted Couscous with Currants and Pine Nuts

Another take on couscous, delicious with the chicken in the Dinner in the Kitchen menu (page 10).

2	14 1/2-ounce cans low-salt chicken broth
6	tablespoons (3/4 stick) butter
3	cups couscous
1/2	cup dried currants
1/2	cup pine nuts, toasted
4	green onions, thinly sliced
1/4	cup minced fresh mint
2	tablespoons minced fresh dill

• Bring broth and butter to boil in medium saucepan. Remove from heat; stir in couscous. Cover; let stand 5 minutes. Fluff couscous with fork. Transfer to bowl. Add currants, pine nuts, green onions, mint and dill; stir to blend. Season with salt and pepper.
• *6 to 8 servings*

Broccoli Puree with Parmesan and Nutmeg

Delicious and different, yet easy—this do-ahead side dish could replace the salad in the Bistro Supper (page 42).

3	pounds broccoli (about 2 large bunches)
6	tablespoons (3/4 stick) unsalted butter, cut up
2/3	cup freshly grated Parmesan cheese
1/4	teaspoon ground nutmeg

• Cut broccoli stems into 1-inch pieces. Cut tops into florets. Bring large pot of salted water to boil. Add broccoli stems and cook 6 minutes. Add broccoli florets and cook until stems and florets are very tender, about 6 more minutes. Drain well. Set aside 10 florets. Place remaining broccoli in processor. Add butter and puree, stopping occasionally to scrape down sides of bowl, about 5 minutes. Blend in grated Parmesan cheese and ground nutmeg. Season to taste with salt and pepper. *(Can be prepared 1 day ahead. Cover and refrigerate 10 florets and broccoli puree separately. Bring florets to room temperature before continuing.)*
• Reheat broccoli puree in saucepan. Garnish with broccoli florets and serve.

• *8 servings*

Baked Tomato Wedges

Just three ingredients in a clever and tasty side dish to serve with the main course in the Dinner and a Movie menu (page 78). You might also try these with the Grand Marnier French Toast on page 143.

	Olive oil
12	plum tomatoes, each cut into quarters
3	tablespoons chopped fresh basil

• Preheat oven to 300°F. Lightly brush heavy large baking sheet with oil. Arrange tomatoes on baking sheet. Lightly brush with oil. Sprinkle basil over. Season with salt and pepper.
• Bake tomatoes until tender, about 30 minutes. Transfer to platter; serve.

• *6 servings*

Cilantro Carrots with Cumin

This light and easy side dish would be a fine addition to the Dinner in the Kitchen menu (page 10).

2	pounds carrots, each cut into 2-inch-long pieces, then quartered lengthwise
6	tablespoons water
3	tablespoons fresh lemon juice
3	tablespoons olive oil
2	tablespoons ground cumin
2	garlic cloves, pressed
2	tablespoons minced fresh cilantro

• Combine carrots and 6 tablespoons water in large saucepan. Season with salt. Cover and boil until carrots are crisp-tender, about 7 minutes. Drain off any excess water. Transfer carrots to large shallow bowl. Mix in lemon juice, oil, cumin and garlic. Season with salt and pepper. Cool. Add cilantro. *(Can be made 2 hours ahead. Let stand at cool room temperature.)*
• *6 to 8 servings*

Roasted New Potatoes with Horseradish and Mustard

A different kind of potato dish, and one that could replace the galette in the Bistro Supper menu (page 42).

3	pounds 1 1/2-inch-diameter red-skinned potatoes, halved
2	tablespoons vegetable oil
2/3	cup finely grated fresh horseradish
1/2	cup coarse Pommery seed mustard*
1/4	cup (1/2 stick) butter, melted

• Preheat oven to 400°F. Brush 2 large baking sheets with oil. Toss potatoes with 2 tablespoons oil in large bowl. Season with salt and pepper. Spread potatoes on baking sheets in single layer. Roast until almost tender, about 30 minutes.
• Meanwhile, combine horseradish, mustard and butter in bowl. Spoon half of mixture over potatoes; toss well. Roast potatoes 15 minutes. Toss potatoes with remaining mustard mixture. Roast until very tender, tossing occasionally, about 10 minutes. Transfer to bowl and serve.
* *Pommery seed mustard is available at specialty foods stores and some supermarkets.*

• *8 servings*

Orzo with Brown Butter and Parsley

A quick pasta dish that goes well with the Roast Turkey with Prosciutto, Rosemary and Garlic on page 132.

9 cups canned low-salt chicken broth
3 cups orzo (rice-shaped pasta; also called riso)

1/2 cup (1 stick) butter
3 garlic cloves, pressed
3/4 teaspoon ground nutmeg
1/2 cup minced fresh parsley

• Pour broth into heavy large saucepan. Bring to boil. Add orzo; boil until tender and liquid is absorbed, stirring often, about 15 minutes. Remove from heat.
• Melt butter in heavy medium skillet over medium-high heat. Stir until butter is golden, about 4 minutes. Remove from heat. Stir in garlic and nutmeg. Pour over orzo. Add parsley. Season with salt and pepper. Transfer to large bowl and serve.

• *10 servings*

Sautéed Green Beans with Shallots and Hazelnuts

This easy sauté of green beans and hazelnuts is fragrant with rosemary. Try it in place of the salad in the Bistro Supper (page 42).

2 pounds green beans, trimmed

1/4 cup (1/2 stick) butter
2/3 cup chopped shallots (about 3 large)
1 teaspoon chopped fresh rosemary or 1 teaspoon dried
1/2 cup hazelnuts, toasted, husked, chopped

• Cook green beans in large pot of boiling salted water until crisp-tender, about 5 minutes. Drain. Rinse green beans with cold water; drain well. Pat dry with paper towels. *(Can be prepared 1 day ahead. Cover beans and refrigerate.)*
• Melt butter in heavy large skillet over medium-high heat. Add shallots and rosemary and sauté until shallots are tender, about 5 minutes. Add green beans and toss until heated through, about 5 minutes. Season to taste with salt and pepper. Add chopped hazelnuts and toss. Transfer to bowl and serve.

• *8 to 10 servings*

Roasted Root Vegetables

Have this as a side dish with the Roast Turkey with Prosciutto, Rosemary and Garlic on page 132.

4 small turnips, peeled, halved, sliced
4 medium parsnips, peeled, sliced
2 large rutabagas, peeled, quartered, sliced
2 yams (red-skinned sweet potatoes), peeled, sliced
1 large acorn squash, peeled, quartered, seeded, cut into 1/3-inch-thick slices
1/2 cup olive oil

• Preheat oven to 425°F. Combine all vegetables in large bowl. Add oil; toss to coat thoroughly. Season with salt and pepper. *(Can be made 2 hours ahead. Cover and let stand at room temperature.)* Arrange vegetables on 2 heavy large baking sheets.
• Roast vegetables until tender and beginning to turn golden brown, stirring occasionally, 50 minutes. Transfer to large bowl and serve.

• *10 servings*

Bulgur with Leeks, Cranberries and Almonds

This simple-to-make side dish would blend in perfectly with the Moroccan dishes in Dinner in the Kitchen (page 10), substituting for the couscous.

6	tablespoons (3/4 stick) butter
3	cups chopped leeks (white and pale green parts only)
5	cups canned low-salt chicken broth
3	cups bulgur*
2/3	cup dried cranberries
2/3	cup sliced almonds, toasted

• Melt butter in heavy large saucepan over medium-high heat. Add chopped leeks and sauté until very tender, about 12 minutes. Add chicken broth and bring to boil. Stir in bulgur and boil 5 minutes. Add dried cranberries. Remove from heat, cover and let stand 15 minutes. Fluff with fork. Mix in sliced almonds. Season to taste with salt and pepper.
* Also called cracked wheat, bulgur is available at natural foods stores and some supermarkets.

• *6 servings*

Sautéed Escarole with White Beans and Tomatoes

Add this deliciously different vegetable side dish to the Dinner and a Movie menu (page 78), replacing the pilaf.

2	heads escarole (about 3 pounds)
3 1/2	tablespoons olive oil
3	garlic cloves, chopped
15	fresh basil leaves, thinly sliced
2	fresh plum tomatoes, seeded, chopped
1	15- to 16-ounce can cannellini (white kidney beans), rinsed, drained

• Rinse escarole under running water. Drain well. Cut into large pieces. Pat dry with paper towels. Heat 1½ tablespoons olive oil in heavy large Dutch oven over medium-high heat. Add garlic and sauté until golden, about 2 minutes. Add ¼ of escarole and sauté until just wilted and beginning to brown, about 3 minutes. Using tongs, transfer escarole to large bowl. Sauté remaining escarole in 3 batches, adding 1 teaspoon olive oil to pot for each batch.
• Heat remaining 1 tablespoon olive oil in same Dutch oven over medium-high heat. Return all escarole to Dutch oven. Add fresh basil, chopped tomatoes and cannellini and stir until heated through, about 5 minutes. Season with salt and pepper. Transfer to large bowl and serve.
• *6 servings*

Creamed Spinach

This recipe is a lower fat version of the classic, made with turkey sausage and half and half. It would be a good addition to the Bistro Supper (page 42).

1	large onion, chopped
3/4	pound turkey Italian sausages, casings removed
3	10-ounce packages frozen chopped spinach, thawed, squeezed dry
1	tablespoon all purpose flour
2	cups canned low-salt chicken broth
1/2	cup half and half
1/2	teaspoon ground nutmeg

• Combine onion and sausages in heavy large Dutch oven over medium heat. Sauté until sausages brown and onion is very tender, breaking up sausages with back of spoon, about 15 minutes. Add spinach; stir until all spinach liquid evaporates, about 4 minutes. Mix in flour; stir 1 minute. Add broth, half and half and nutmeg. Simmer until mixture is thick, stirring frequently, about 10 minutes. Season with salt and pepper.
• *8 servings*

the potluck

Menu for Twelve	Crudités and Grilled Sausages with Sweet and Hot Chutneys (page 107)
	Roast Beef Tenderloin with Horseradish-Chive Sauce (page 138)
	Potato, Roasted Pepper and Arugula Salad (page 117)
	Green Bean and Tomato Salad (page 117)
	Blue Cheese Bread (page 109)
	Dry Red Wine
	Mandarin Chocolate Cake (page 156)
	Coffee and Tea

It's a common refrain among busy people: It would be great if we could all get together sometime...We should have a party when this is over...It's been fun working with you, and the kids get along so well.... ★ As many reasons as there are for socializing with a large group of people —colleagues, team members, a parents' group, perhaps — there is always that one big reason not to: It's a lot of work. A potluck, an old idea that seems new again in these frantic days of the late twentieth century, is the ideal solution. ★ As simple as the basic premise of a potluck is — everybody gathers at someone's house, bringing a dish of their own making — success depends on some planning. This menu addresses the three main potluck priorities: dishes that complement each other in flavor and texture, food that can travel, and recipes that require little, if any, last-minute work. ★ Here, the spectrum of tastes is delightful: two zingy chutneys with vegetable and sausage dippers; beef tenderloin with a creamy horseradish sauce; potato salad with Mediterranean accents; green beans with a mustard dressing; French bread toasted with blue cheese butter; and a very chocolaty cake with hints of ginger and orange. The only last-minute tasks are reheating the sausages, which can be done fast in the microwave, and running the bread under the broiler. ★ All it takes, really, is a decision to do it. Then set the time and place and divide up the recipes. You'll be glad you did.

mix-and-match main courses

poultry

Chicken with Mild Red Chili Sauce

This sophisticated dish is surprisingly simple to prepare. If there's a grill where you're going, pack the chicken up for the Picnic in the Country (page 48); the salads in the menu will go nicely with it.

3/4	cup fresh lemon juice
3/4	cup dry white wine
6	tablespoons olive oil
4 1/2	tablespoons California chili powder*
9	garlic cloves, chopped
3	shallots, chopped
2	tablespoons soy sauce
2	tablespoons honey
1 1/2	tablespoons fresh oregano leaves or 1 1/2 teaspoons dried
8	large boneless chicken breast halves with skin

Oregano sprigs (optional)

• Puree first 9 ingredients in blender until smooth. Using meat mallet, pound chicken breasts between sheets of plastic wrap to ½-inch thickness. Place chicken in 13 x 9 x 2-inch glass baking dish. Pour marinade over and turn to coat. Cover and refrigerate chicken overnight.

• Prepare barbecue (medium-high heat) or preheat broiler. Drain marinade into small saucepan. Boil 5 minutes. Season chicken with salt and pepper.

• Grill or broil chicken until cooked through, about 5 minutes per side. Brush some marinade over chicken. Transfer to platter. Garnish with oregano sprigs, if desired. Serve with remaining marinade.

A mild red chili powder available in the spice section of some supermarkets. If unavailable, use regular mild chili powder.

• *8 servings*

Chicken Breasts Stuffed with Mushrooms and Spinach

Here, an innovative stuffing of sautéed spinach, mushrooms and ground almonds is placed under the skin of the chicken breasts. Make the "packages" ahead, then bake just before serving. Easy *and* impressive. These would work in the Lunch on the Terrace menu (page 28), with two extras for hearty appetites (or even lunch the next day).

1/2   cup (1 stick) butter, room temperature
4   garlic cloves, minced
1   tablespoon chopped fresh parsley
1/2   teaspoon dried crushed red pepper

1 1/2   cups chopped mushrooms (about 4 1/2 ounces)
1 1/2   cups chopped fresh spinach
3/4   cup finely ground almonds (about 3 ounces)
1/2   cup sour cream

6   boneless chicken breast halves with skin

• Mix first 4 ingredients in small bowl until smooth. Season garlic butter to taste with salt and pepper. *(Can be prepared 1 day ahead. Cover and refrigerate. Bring to room temperature before using.)*
• Melt 2 tablespoons garlic butter in heavy large skillet over medium-high heat. Add mushrooms and sauté until tender and all liquid evaporates, about 3 minutes. Add spinach; sauté until just wilted, about 1 minute. Transfer mixture to medium bowl. Cool 30 minutes. Stir in almonds and sour cream. Season with salt and pepper.
• Run fingers between chicken skin and meat to loosen (do not remove skin). Spread 2 teaspoons garlic butter under skin over meat of each chicken breast. Spoon 2 generous tablespoons stuffing under skin of each chicken breast. Using toothpicks, skewer skin to chicken to enclose stuffing. Arrange chicken on large baking sheet. Spread remaining garlic butter over top of each chicken breast. *(Can be prepared 4 hours ahead. Cover and refrigerate.)*
• Preheat oven to 350°F. Bake until chicken is cooked through, about 30 minutes. Transfer chicken to platter.
• *6 servings*

Easy Chicken Pot Pies

These old-fashioned chicken pies are ready in a nineties flash—and they make perfect TV dinner fare, especially when TV is a good video, as in the Dinner and a Movie menu (page 78).

3   refrigerated pie crusts (1 1/2 15-ounce packages), room temperature

6   tablespoons all purpose flour
4 1/2   teaspoons dried rubbed sage
24   ounces skinless boneless chicken breasts, cut into 1-inch pieces
4 1/2   tablespoons butter
4   cups canned chicken broth
4 1/2   cups frozen mixed vegetables

• Preheat oven to 425°F. Place crusts on work surface. Press out fold lines; pinch to seal any cracks. Cut out 6 pastry rounds to fit tops of six 2-cup ramekins. Arrange crusts on baking sheet. Pierce with fork. Bake crusts until golden, about 8 minutes.
• Meanwhile, combine flour and 1½ teaspoons sage in medium bowl. Season chicken with salt and pepper. Add chicken to flour; toss to coat. Melt butter in heavy large Dutch oven over medium-high heat. Add chicken and any remaining flour to Dutch oven and stir until chicken is brown, about 10 minutes. Mix in broth, vegetables and 3 teaspoons sage. Bring to boil, scraping up any browned bits. Reduce heat, cover and simmer until chicken is cooked through, about 8 minutes. Season with salt and pepper.
• Transfer filling to ramekins, dividing evenly. Top with crusts and serve.
• *6 servings*

Chicken with Mild Red Chili Sauce; Cilantro Carrots with Cumin (page 123); and Minted Couscous with Currants and Pine Nuts (page 122)

Roast Pesto Chicken

If you've planned on Lunch on the Terrace (page 28), but the weather doesn't cooperate, this easy roast chicken recipe (in which pesto, that thick basil, pine nut and Parmesan sauce, is spread under the skin before cooking) would make a fine, cool-weather dish to replace the chicken salad. Roasted potato wedges and steamed broccoli would be good, simple go-withs.

1   6 1/2- to 7-pound roasting chicken
1   7-ounce container purchased pesto sauce

3   tablespoons dry white wine
3/4   cup (about) plus 2 tablespoons canned low-salt chicken broth
2   tablespoons all purpose flour
3   tablespoons whipping cream
    Fresh basil sprigs

• Pat chicken dry. Slide hand between chicken skin and meat over breast and legs to form pockets. Reserve 1 tablespoon pesto for gravy; spread remaining pesto under skin and over breast and leg meat of chicken, in cavity of chicken and over outer skin. Tie legs together to hold shape. Tuck wings under body. Place chicken in large roasting pan. *(Can be made 4 hours ahead. Cover and chill.)*

• Preheat oven to 450°F. Roast chicken 15 minutes. Reduce oven temperature to 375°F and roast until juices run clear when chicken is pierced in thickest part of thigh, basting occasionally with pan juices, about 1 hour 15 minutes. Transfer chicken to platter.

• Pour pan juices into glass measuring cup; degrease. Add wine to roasting pan and bring to boil, scraping up any browned bits. Add wine mixture and any drippings from platter to pan juices. Add enough broth to measure 1 cup. Transfer to heavy small saucepan. Combine 2 tablespoons broth and flour in bowl; stir until smooth. Add to saucepan. Bring to boil, whisking constantly. Boil until reduced to sauce consistency, stirring often, about 5 minutes. Mix in cream and reserved 1 tablespoon pesto. Season with salt and pepper. Garnish chicken with basil. Serve with gravy.

• *4 servings*

Roast Pesto Chicken (far left);
Chicken, Black Bean and Goat
Cheese Tostadas (left)

Chicken, Black Bean and Goat Cheese Tostadas

Lighten up the South-of-the-Border Party menu (page 84) by offering these streamlined tostadas in place of the enchiladas and chicken salad.

BEANS

- 2 tablespoons olive oil
- 1 red onion, chopped
- 2 large jalapeño chilies, seeded but not deveined, minced
- 1 teaspoon chili powder
- 1/2 teaspoon ground cumin
- 2 16-ounce cans black beans, rinsed, drained
- 2 tablespoons fresh lime juice

CHICKEN

- 2 tablespoons olive oil
- 1 1/2 pounds boneless chicken breasts, skinned, cut into 3/4-inch pieces
- 1 1/2 teaspoons chili powder
- 3/4 teaspoon ground cumin

SALAD

- 4 cups sliced romaine lettuce
- 1 medium head radicchio, sliced
- 1/2 cup fresh cilantro leaves

Vegetable oil
- 6 corn tortillas

- 1/4 cup olive oil
- 1 tablespoon fresh lime juice
- 2 tablespoons (about) water
- 1/2 pound goat cheese, crumbled
  Avocado Salsa (see recipe at right)
- 6 fresh cilantro sprigs

• FOR BEANS: Heat olive oil in heavy medium saucepan over medium-low heat. Add onion and chilies; cook until onion is translucent, stirring occasionally, about 8 minutes. Add chili powder and cumin; stir 30 seconds. Add beans and lime juice. Cook until heated through, stirring and mashing beans slightly with spoon, about 4 minutes. *(Can be prepared 1 day ahead. Cover and chill.)*

• FOR CHICKEN: Heat oil in heavy large skillet over high heat. Add chicken and sprinkle with salt and pepper. Stir until almost cooked through, about 3 minutes. Add chili powder and cumin and stir until cooked through, about 30 seconds. Remove from heat.
• FOR SALAD: Combine first 3 ingredients in large bowl. Set aside.
• Add oil to depth of 1/4 inch to heavy medium skillet. Heat over medium-high heat until just beginning to smoke. Add tortilla and cook until crisp, about 30 seconds per side. Drain on paper towels. Repeat with remaining tortillas.
• Add 1/4 cup olive oil to salad; toss. Season with salt and pepper. Add 1 tablespoon lime juice; toss. Rewarm beans over medium-low heat, stirring and thinning slightly with water. Place 1 tortilla on each plate. Spread with beans. Sprinkle with cheese. Top with salad, then chicken, salsa and cilantro.
• *6 servings*

Avocado Salsa

- 2 large tomatoes, seeded, diced
- 1/2 red onion, chopped
- 1/2 cup chopped fresh cilantro
- 1/4 cup olive oil
- 2 tablespoons fresh lime juice
- 1 to 2 large jalapeño chilies, seeded but not deveined, minced
- 1 large avocado, diced

• Combine first 6 ingredients in medium bowl. Season with salt. *(Can be prepared 2 hours ahead. Cover and refrigerate.)* Add avocado to salsa just before serving.
• *Makes about 4 cups*

Three-Cheese Chicken Breasts in Tomato Sauce

The terrific thing about this dish is that the components—chicken breasts, tomato sauce and pasta—all get cooked ahead; then it's a simple matter of layering them in a dish, topping with cheese and baking for 20 minutes. A casserole for the nineties. Try this recipe in place of the scampi and pilaf in the Dinner and a Movie menu (page 78).

- 1/4 cup olive oil
- 6 skinless boneless chicken breast halves
- 1/2 large onion, chopped
- 2 large garlic cloves, chopped
- 1 tablespoon dried oregano
- 1 15-ounce can tomato sauce
- 1 14 1/2-ounce can Italian-style stewed tomatoes
- 1/3 cup dry white wine
- 2 bay leaves

- 8 ounces penne, freshly cooked
- 1 cup grated mozzarella cheese
- 1/3 cup grated Asiago or Romano cheese
- 1/3 cup freshly grated Parmesan cheese

• Preheat oven to 375°F. Butter 13 x 9 x 2-inch glass baking dish. Heat oil in heavy large skillet over high heat. Season chicken with salt and pepper. Add chicken to skillet; sauté until outside is white, about 1 minute per side; transfer to plate. Add onion, garlic and oregano to skillet and sauté until onion begins to soften, about 4 minutes. Add tomato sauce, stewed tomatoes with their juices, wine and bay leaves and cook until sauce thickens, breaking up tomatoes with spoon, about 8 minutes; discard bay leaves.
• Line prepared dish with penne. Arrange chicken over. Spoon sauce over, covering chicken and pasta completely. Mix cheeses in small bowl. Sprinkle cheeses over sauce. Bake until chicken is just cooked through and sauce bubbles, about 20 minutes. Serve hot.
• *6 servings*

Roast Turkey with Prosciutto, Rosemary and Garlic

A mixture of prosciutto, rosemary and garlic rubbed under the skin of the turkey gives it a distinctively delicious taste. For a Family Reunion (page 64) of a different kind, offer this beautiful bird with the Roasted Root Vegetables on page 124, the Orzo with Brown Butter and Parsley on page 124, a salad to start, some steamed spinach alongside, and the Raspberry and Marsala Trifle on page 162 for dessert.

    1   18- to 20-pound turkey
    4   tablespoons plus 1/2 teaspoon
        minced fresh rosemary
    4   tablespoons chopped garlic
    8   ounces thinly sliced prosciutto,
        chopped

        Olive oil
    3   whole heads garlic, each cut in
        half horizontally
    2   cups (or more) canned low-salt
        chicken broth

    1/2 cup dry white wine

    3 1/2 tablespoons all purpose flour

        Fresh rosemary sprigs

• Pat turkey dry. Run hands under skin of turkey, separating skin from breast and thighs. Rub 3 tablespoons rosemary and 3 tablespoons garlic under skin over breast and thighs. Carefully arrange half of prosciutto under skin over breast and thighs. Rub 1 tablespoon rosemary and 1 tablespoon garlic inside cavity of turkey. Sprinkle remaining prosciutto into cavity. Place turkey in heavy large roasting pan. Cover with plastic and chill overnight.

• Preheat oven to 450°F. Rub outside of turkey with oil. Season with pepper. Place 1 head of garlic in cavity of turkey. Place 2 heads of garlic in roasting pan. Tie turkey legs together. Roast turkey 30 minutes. Reduce oven temperature to 325°F. Continue roasting turkey until thermometer inserted into thickest part of thigh registers 180°F, basting occasionally with 2 cups broth, about 3 hours. Transfer turkey to platter. Surround with roasted garlic and garlic from turkey cavity. Remove prosciutto from turkey cavity; reserve. Tent turkey with foil to keep warm.

• Pour pan juices into large glass measuring cup. Skim fat from surface of pan juices, reserving 3 tablespoons fat. Set roasting pan over medium-high heat. Add wine and bring to boil, scraping up any browned bits. Add wine mixture to pan juices in cup (liquids should measure 2½ cups; if not, add more broth or boil until reduced to 2½ cups).

• Heat reserved 3 tablespoons fat in heavy medium saucepan over medium heat. Add flour; stir until golden, about 2 minutes. Whisk in pan juices. Mix in ½ teaspoon rosemary. Boil until thickened to sauce consistency, stirring occasionally, about 5 minutes. Mix in reserved prosciutto. Garnish turkey with rosemary sprigs. Serve with gravy.

• *10 servings*

*Roast Turkey with Prosciutto, Rosemary and Garlic (below left);
Smoked Turkey and Watercress Sandwiches (below right)*

Smoked Turkey and Watercress Sandwiches

The idea behind the Pizza Party (page 70) could easily be translated into other kinds of foods—sandwiches, for instance. Try these do-it-yourself sandwiches with the crudités, the salad and the dessert for an easy lunch.

6 to 8 pita bread rounds

1 1/2	pounds sliced smoked turkey
2	watercress bunches, trimmed
8	plum tomatoes, sliced
1	cup walnuts, chopped
	Curried Apricot Mayonnaise (see recipe below)

• Preheat oven to 350°F. Place pita bread on baking sheet and heat in oven until just warm, about 5 minutes. Cut rounds in half, forming pockets. Place in napkin-lined basket and keep warm.
• Arrange turkey, watercress and tomatoes on platter. Place walnuts and curried mayonnaise in bowls; allow diners to assemble their own sandwiches.
• *6 to 8 servings*

Curried Apricot Mayonnaise

1 1/2	cups mayonnaise
1/4	cup apricot jam
1 1/2	teaspoons curry powder

• Whisk ingredients in medium bowl to blend well. *(Can be prepared 2 days ahead. Cover with plastic and refrigerate.)*
• *Makes about 1 ¾ cups*

Turkey Tenderloins with Romesco Sauce

In this classic dish, marinated grilled turkey breast gets topped with a rich sauce of roasted red peppers, garlic and almonds. Try it as the main course in the Garden Party menu (page 92).

SAUCE

6	medium-size red bell peppers, halved lengthwise, seeded
6	garlic cloves
1/3	cup slivered blanched almonds, toasted
1	tablespoon grated lemon peel
1/4	teaspoon cayenne pepper
1/2	cup olive oil

TURKEY

1	cup olive oil
6	garlic cloves, minced
2	teaspoons dried thyme
1	teaspoon dried oregano
1/8	teaspoon cayenne pepper
4	3/4-pound turkey breast tenderloins

• FOR SAUCE: Preheat broiler. Place peppers skin side up on broiler pan. Broil until skins are entirely blackened. Transfer peppers to paper bag and seal. Let stand 10 minutes to steam. Peel and seed peppers; cut into large pieces.
• Finely chop garlic in processor. Add peppers, almonds, lemon peel and cayenne and blend until as smooth as possible. Gradually blend in oil. Season to taste with salt and pepper. Cover and refrigerate overnight. *(Can be prepared 2 days ahead. Bring to room temperature before serving.)*
• FOR TURKEY: Mix first 5 ingredients in small bowl. Place turkey in shallow baking dish. Pour marinade over and turn to coat. Cover and chill 4 hours.
• Prepare barbecue (medium heat). Remove turkey from marinade; reserve marinade. Season turkey with salt and pepper. Place turkey on grill and cook 5 minutes, turning once. Cover loosely with foil and grill until turkey is cooked through, turning occasionally and basting with marinade, about 12 minutes more. Transfer to platter. Tent with foil and let stand 5 minutes. Cut turkey crosswise into slices. Arrange on platter. Serve, passing sauce separately.
• *8 servings*

Turkey Tenderloins with Romesco Sauce

seafood

Salmon Fillets with Lemon-Thyme Sauce

You might serve this elegant dish instead of the chicken salad in the Lunch on the Terrace menu (page 28).

    4   6-ounce salmon fillets

1/2   cup dry white wine
1/2   cup whipping cream
1/2   cup chopped shallots (about 6)
    1   tablespoon white wine vinegar
1/2   teaspoon dried thyme
    6   tablespoons (3/4 stick) chilled unsalted butter, cut into 6 pieces
1 1/2   teaspoons fresh lemon juice

• Preheat oven to 375°F. Arrange salmon on baking sheet and season with salt and pepper. Bake until just cooked through, about 20 minutes.
• Meanwhile, boil next 5 ingredients in heavy medium saucepan over high heat until mixture is reduced to generous ½ cup, stirring occasionally, about 12 minutes. Strain sauce into heavy small saucepan, pushing hard on solids to release as much liquid as possible. Set saucepan over very low heat and whisk in butter 1 piece at a time. Whisk in lemon juice; season sauce to taste with salt and pepper.
• Transfer salmon to plates. Spoon sauce over and serve immediately.
• *4 servings*

Grilled Tuna with Olive-Rosemary Butter

In keeping with the French theme of the Bistro Supper (page 42), this simple, sunny dish has all the flavors of the south of France and works well with the rest of the dishes in the menu.

1/2   cup (1 stick) unsalted butter, room temperature
    2   tablespoons chopped pitted brine-cured black olives (such as Kalamata)
1/2   teaspoon plus 2 tablespoons fresh lemon juice
    4   teaspoons chopped fresh rosemary or 1 teaspoon dried
1/2   teaspoon Dijon mustard

    6   tablespoons olive oil
1/4   teaspoon pepper
    8   8-ounce tuna steaks (1 inch thick)

        Fresh rosemary sprigs (optional)

• Blend butter, olives, ½ teaspoon lemon juice, 2 teaspoons rosemary and mustard in small bowl. (*Butter can be prepared up to 2 days ahead. Wrap tightly and refrigerate. Let stand at room temperature 45 minutes.*)
• Whisk olive oil with remaining 2 tablespoons fresh lemon juice, remaining 2 teaspoons rosemary and pepper in large shallow dish. Arrange tuna steaks in dish, turning to coat. Let stand 15 minutes.
• Prepare barbecue (high heat). Grill tuna until just cooked through, about 4 minutes per side. Transfer to platter. Place 1 tablespoon rosemary butter on each steak. Garnish with rosemary sprigs.
• *8 servings*

Shrimp and Potatoes with Garlic and Saffron (far left); Lobster Salad with Green Beans, Corn and Bell Pepper (left)

Shrimp and Potatoes with Garlic and Saffron

While the dishes in the Dinner in the Kitchen menu (page 10) revolve around a Moroccan theme, many of them will work equally well in any menu of Mediterranean origin. Try this Spanish sauté of shrimp and potatoes in place of the chicken and couscous.

1 1/2   pounds baby red potatoes, quartered
2   cups dry white wine
3/8   teaspoon saffron threads

1/3   cup olive oil
12   large garlic cloves, minced
3   pounds uncooked jumbo shrimp (about 10 to 12 per pound), peeled, deveined
1/4   teaspoon dried crushed red pepper
3   tablespoons tomato paste
1   10-ounce package frozen baby peas, thawed
2   teaspoons dried marjoram

• Cook potatoes in large saucepan of boiling water until just tender. Drain. Combine wine and saffron in bowl.
• Heat oil in heavy large skillet over medium-low heat. Add garlic and sauté until just beginning to color, about 3 minutes. Add shrimp and dried red pepper; increase heat to medium-high and stir to coat shrimp with oil. Add tomato paste and wine mixture. Bring to boil, stirring constantly. Cook until shrimp are just tender, about 5 minutes. Transfer shrimp to bowl, using slotted spoon. Add potatoes to skillet and boil until liquid thickens to sauce consistency, about 6 minutes. Return shrimp and any juices in bowl to skillet. Mix in peas and marjoram and heat through. Season with salt and pepper and serve.
• *6 servings*

Lobster Salad with Green Beans, Corn and Bell Pepper

Turn the afternoon you have planned for the Garden Party (page 92) into a real occasion by serving this centerpiece salad of lobster, corn and bell pepper in place of the fish, salad and corn.

SALAD
4   cups fresh green beans, cut into 1-inch pieces
4   cups fresh corn kernels or frozen, thawed
2   large red bell peppers, cut into matchstick-size strips
1/2   cup diced onion

DRESSING
6   tablespoons tarragon vinegar
4   teaspoons cracked black pepper
3   tablespoons coarse-grained mustard
2   tablespoons honey
1 1/2   cups vegetable oil
6   tablespoons finely chopped fresh tarragon or 4 teaspoons dried

8   cooked lobster tails
  Small butter lettuce leaves or lamb's lettuce
  Lemon wedges

• FOR SALAD: Bring large saucepan of salted water to boil. Add green beans and cook until just tender, about 2 minutes. Transfer to bowl of ice water using slotted spoon and cool. Return water to boil. Add corn kernels and cook until just tender, about 3 minutes. Drain. Transfer to bowl of ice water and cool. Drain green beans and corn. Transfer to large bowl. Add bell pepper and diced onion and set aside.

• FOR DRESSING: Bring vinegar and pepper to simmer in heavy small saucepan. Whisk in mustard and honey. Remove from heat. Gradually whisk in oil. Mix in tarragon. Pour half of dressing over vegetables in bowl. Let stand 1 hour at room temperature.
• Slice each lobster tail into medallions and fan on 1 side of each plate. Spoon vegetable salad in center of plates. Garnish with lettuce and lemon wedges. Serve, passing remaining dressing separately.
• *8 servings*

Shrimp and Scallop Sauté

Sticking to the seafood theme of the Dinner and a Movie menu (page 78), replace the scampi with this quick sauté of shrimp and scallops.

3   tablespoons butter
3   tablespoons olive oil
6   large garlic cloves, minced
1   pound mushrooms, sliced
2   tablespoons tomato paste
1/4   cup dry white wine
1/4   cup fresh lemon juice
1   pound medium shrimp, peeled, deveined
1   bunch green onions, sliced
1   pound bay scallops
1/3   cup chopped fresh parsley

• Melt butter with olive oil in heavy large skillet over medium heat. Add minced garlic cloves and sauté 1 minute. Increase heat to high, add sliced mushrooms and sauté until just beginning to soften, about 5 minutes. Add tomato paste and stir 30 seconds. Add dry white wine and fresh lemon juice and bring to boil. Add shrimp and sliced green onions and stir 1 minute. Add scallops and stir until shrimp and scallops are cooked through, about 3 minutes. Season to taste with salt and pepper. Sprinkle with chopped fresh parsley and serve immediately.
• *6 servings*

Menu Basics

Devising a menu of your own design from the many recipes here isn't difficult—it's a simple matter of remembering some basic elements of menu planning. Keep the following in mind, and you'll be guaranteed a well-rounded, attractive, delicious meal.

If the first course is rich or smooth and creamy, choose a fruit dessert. Conversely, if the dessert you want to serve is quite rich, start with a salad or crudités and a dip.

If the main course is intricately seasoned or spicy, bracket it with the straightforward tastes of, say, a tossed salad and a creamy dessert.

Avoid juggling the typical three elements of a main course—meat, starch and vegetable—by moving the vegetable to the first course, either as a salad, a cooked vegetable, such as asparagus or a whole artichoke, or a light soup.

Anticipate the colors on a plate. When there is no vegetable on the main course plate, add a simple brightener, such as thawed frozen peas stirred into rice, or halved cherry tomatoes and a sprig of dill to go with steak and potatoes. With simple soups and desserts, which are often naturally pale, you can ensure visual interest by using dramatically colored and patterned bowls or plates.

Don't overlook bread. Not only is good bread a favorite food of many, but it's an important source of nutrients. And it comes in all kinds of textures and tastes—from crisp flat breads to crusty rolls to soft muffins. Assemble several kinds in a basket for an enticing centerpiece.

Buy one course if you don't have time to prepare all three (first, main and dessert). Delis offer such first-course possibilities as guacamole you can scoop onto sliced tomatoes, and cooked shrimp and marinated vegetables for an attractive plate duo. Bakery desserts are unlimited. But even take-out pizza or barbecued ribs need no apology, especially if served with a big salad and a homemade dessert.

Seafood Quiche

If you're planning to serve this as the main course of a brunch (like the one on page 112), make the crust ahead, then fill and bake it just before serving. Alternatively, cut the quiche into small squares and offer them as appetizers in the Cocktails at Five menu (page 18).

CRUST
1 1/4	cups all purpose flour
1/4	teaspoon salt
1/4	cup (1/2 stick) chilled unsalted butter, cut into pieces
1/4	cup chilled solid vegetable shortening, cut into pieces
4	tablespoons (about) ice water

FILLING
1 1/2	tablespoons butter
3	shallots, minced
1/2	pound medium uncooked shrimp, peeled, deveined
1/3	pound bay scallops, connective tissue removed
1	cup cooked crabmeat
1	cup whipping cream
1/2	cup milk
1/2	cup minced fresh Italian parsley
3	large eggs
2	egg yolks
1	teaspoon minced fresh tarragon or 1/4 teaspoon dried
1	teaspoon grated lemon peel
1	teaspoon salt
1/4	teaspoon pepper
1 1/4	cups packed grated Monterey Jack cheese (about 5 ounces)

• FOR CRUST: Combine flour and salt in processor. Add chilled unsalted butter and shortening and blend in using on/off turns until mixture resembles coarse meal. Mix in enough water by tablespoons until dough begins to clump together. Gather dough into ball; flatten into disk. Wrap tightly in plastic and refrigerate 30 minutes. *(Dough can be prepared up to 1 day ahead.)*

• Preheat oven to 375°F. Roll out dough on floured surface to 15 x 12-inch rectangle. Transfer dough to 12 x 7½ x 1½-inch glass baking dish, pressing dough up sides. Trim and crimp edges decoratively. Freeze crust 15 minutes. Line crust with foil. Fill with dried beans or pie weights. Bake until sides are set, about 15 minutes. Remove foil and beans and bake crust until golden brown, about 15 minutes more. Cool. *(Crust can be prepared 1 day ahead. Let stand at room temperature.)*

• FOR FILLING: Preheat oven to 375°F. Melt butter in heavy large skillet over medium heat. Add minced shallots and sauté 3 minutes. Add shrimp and scallops and sauté 2 minutes. Mix in crabmeat. Transfer seafood mixture to sieve and let drain. Whisk whipping cream, milk, minced parsley, whole eggs, 2 egg yolks, minced fresh tarragon, grated lemon peel, salt and pepper in large bowl to blend. Mix in seafood mixture and Monterey Jack cheese.

• Ladle filling into crust. Bake until custard is set, about 45 minutes. Cool 20 minutes. Cut into squares and serve.

• *8 servings*

Grilled Tuna with Mango Salad

Quick and colorful, this dish would make a lovely main course for the Lunch on the Terrace menu (page 28).

1	large mango, pitted, peeled, cut into 1/4-inch-wide strips
3/4	cup chopped red onion
1/2	red bell pepper, chopped
3	tablespoons chopped fresh cilantro
2	tablespoons rice vinegar
2	tablespoons olive oil
4	6-ounce tuna steaks (about 1 inch thick) Vegetable oil

• Mix first 6 ingredients in medium bowl. Season with salt and pepper.
• Prepare barbecue (medium-high heat) or preheat broiler. Brush tuna with oil. Grill or broil until just opaque in center, about 4 minutes per side.
• Divide mango salad among 4 plates. Top with tuna and serve.

• *4 servings*

meats

Grilled Flank Steak with Rosemary

Here's a deliciously simple marinade for flank steak that flavors the meat in only two hours. Then, just grill and serve. Try this in place of the salmon in the Back-Yard Barbecue (page 56).

1/2	cup soy sauce
1/2	cup olive oil
4 1/2	tablespoons honey
6	large garlic cloves, minced
3	tablespoons chopped fresh rosemary or 1 tablespoon dried
1 1/2	tablespoons coarsely ground black pepper
1 1/2	teaspoons salt
1	2 1/4-pound flank steak

• Mix all ingredients except steak in 13 x 9 x 2-inch glass baking dish. Add steak and turn to coat. Cover and refrigerate 2 hours, turning occasionally.
• Prepare barbecue (medium-high heat) or preheat broiler. Remove meat from marinade; discard marinade. Grill steak to desired doneness, about 4 minutes per side for medium-rare.
• Transfer steak to work surface. Let stand 5 minutes. Cut across grain into thin strips. Arrange on platter and serve.

• *6 servings*

Grilled Tuna with Mango Salad

Roast Beef Tenderloin with Horseradish-Chive Sauce

Sophisticated *and* simple, this terrific dish is perfect for entertaining, as it can be made entirely ahead. It's the centerpiece of The Potluck menu on page 126, and it would also star in the Picnic in the Country menu (page 48), though you may have leftovers—not necessarily a bad thing in this case.

2	3-pound beef tenderloin pieces
2	tablespoons dried rosemary
3	tablespoons cracked pepper

1/4	cup soy sauce
1/4	cup (1/2 stick) butter, room temperature

    Kale
    Horseradish-Chive Sauce
    (see recipe at right)

• Rub beef all over with dried rosemary and cracked pepper. Let stand 2 hours at room temperature.
• Preheat oven to 500°F. Brush beef tenderloin pieces with soy sauce; rub with butter. Place tenderloin pieces on rack in roasting pan. Transfer to oven, reduce temperature to 400°F and roast until thermometer inserted into thickest part of meat registers 120°F for rare, about 40 minutes. Cool completely. Refrigerate beef until well chilled. *(Beef can be prepared 1 day ahead. Cover with plastic and keep refrigerated.)*
• Slice beef thinly. Line serving platter with kale. Arrange beef slices atop kale. Serve beef chilled or at room temperature, passing Horseradish-Chive Sauce separately.
• *12 servings*

Horseradish-Chive Sauce

1 1/2	cups mayonnaise or low-fat mayonnaise
1 1/2	cups sour cream or plain yogurt
1/3	cup chopped fresh chives or green onions
1/4	cup prepared horseradish
1/4	cup drained capers

• Combine all ingredients in medium bowl. Season with generous amount of pepper. *(Can be prepared 1 day ahead. Cover with plastic and refrigerate.)*
• *Makes about 4 cups*

Grilled Hamburgers with Sour Cream and Herbs

Sour cream makes these burgers especially moist, and a mix of fresh herbs makes them extra flavorful. They're center-stage in The Cookout on page 148; you could also grill them up for the Garden Party (page 92).

2 2/3	pounds lean ground beef
1/4	cup sour cream
1	tablespoon minced fresh thyme or 1 teaspoon dried
1	tablespoon minced fresh parsley
1	teaspoon minced fresh rosemary or 1/4 teaspoon dried
3/4	teaspoon pepper

8	hamburger buns

    Grilled Red Onions (see recipe on page 121)
    Three-Pepper Ketchup (see recipe on page 139)

• Thoroughly combine first 6 ingredients in medium bowl. Shape beef mixture into eight 1-inch-thick patties. Cover and chill at least 1 hour and up to 8 hours.

• Prepare barbecue (medium-high heat). Place burgers on grill. Cover grill and cook burgers 4 minutes. Turn burgers. Cover grill and cook burgers to desired doneness, about 4 minutes for medium-rare. Grill buns, cut side down, during last 2 minutes if desired.

• Arrange burgers on bottom halves of buns. Cover burgers with bun tops and serve with Grilled Red Onions and Three-Pepper Ketchup.

• *8 servings*

Three-Pepper Ketchup

2	tablespoons olive oil
1/2	cup minced onion
1/2	cup sliced green onions
1/2	cup minced red bell pepper
3	canned pickled jalapeño chilies, stemmed, minced
2	garlic cloves, minced
1/4	teaspoon dried thyme
1 1/2	cups ketchup
3/4	cup canned crushed tomatoes in heavy puree
1/2	teaspoon pepper

• Heat oil in heavy medium saucepan over low heat. Add all onions, bell pepper, chilies, garlic and thyme. Cover and cook until vegetables are tender, stirring occasionally, about 10 minutes. Mix in ketchup, tomatoes and pepper. Cover partially and simmer until thickened, stirring occasionally, about 5 minutes. Cover and chill. *(Can be prepared 2 weeks ahead.)*

• *Makes about 2 ¾ cups*

Fiesta Fajitas

Make these the centerpiece of a big party (see the Easy Guacamole on page 102 for details). Set out baskets of warm tortillas and bowls of guacamole and the Pico de Gallo here (a spicy, fresh salsa) so that guests can assemble their own fajitas.

4 1/2	cups fresh lime juice (about 25 large limes)
4 1/2	cups soy sauce
4 1/2	cups Worcestershire sauce
9	pounds beef skirt steaks, fat trimmed, cut in half crosswise
5	green bell peppers, quartered
5	red bell peppers, quartered
4 1/2	onions, cut into 1/2-inch-thick rounds
72	(about) warm flour tortillas Easy Guacamole (see recipe on page 102) Pico de Gallo (see recipe at right)

• Place lime juice in large bowl. Gradually whisk in soy and Worcestershire sauces. Transfer to large roasting pan. Add steaks, bell peppers and onions and turn to coat. Cover tightly. Refrigerate 2 hours, turning steaks occasionally.

• Prepare barbecue (medium-high heat). Drain steaks, bell peppers and onions. Place on grill. Cook until steaks are medium-rare and bell peppers and onions are tender and lightly charred, turning steaks, bell peppers and onions occasionally, about 10 minutes.

• Transfer steaks, bell peppers and onions to cutting board. Cut steaks diagonally across grain into thin slices. Cut bell peppers into strips. Halve onions to separate rings. Mound steak, bell peppers and onions on large platter. Serve with warm flour tortillas, guacamole and Pico de Gallo.

• *24 servings*

Pico de Gallo

6	cups drained chopped tomatoes (about 6 large)
3	medium onions, finely chopped
1 1/2	cups chopped fresh cilantro
6	jalapeño chilies, seeded, finely chopped

• Mix all ingredients in large bowl. Season to taste with salt and pepper. *(Can be prepared 3 hours ahead. Cover and let stand at room temperature.)*

• *Makes about 10 cups*

Setting A Place

There is no mystery to the traditional place setting: Positioned about one inch from the edge of the table, the dinner plate is topped by the salad plate, with the bread-and-butter plate to the left above the forks and utensils placed in order of usage, outside to in. The water goblet goes directly above the tip of the knife on the right, the wine glass to the right of it, and the flute behind. And for a formal occasion, this may be just how you want to set the table. For the casual occasion, though, maybe a little mystery is what's called for. Here are some ways to add interest to the table.

If you're fond of picking up unusual, unmatched dinner plates at yard sales and such, use them as serving plates, leaving them under the first course and removing them before serving the entrée.

Mix china and flatware patterns. Each place setting can be different, or you can alternate patterns (a useful design scheme when you don't have enough of a single pattern to go around).

Don't limit yourself to tablecloths and place mats. Look to sheets, pieces of fabric, lengths of lace, scarves, quilts, even bedspreads to top the table.

Experiment with layers of table coverings, mixing and matching to find complementary juxtapositions of color and texture. Top a classic white tablecloth with a stretch of gauzy silk chiffon; arrange napkins, with one corner toward the center and the other draping over the table edge, atop a cloth in a contrasting color.

Don't forget the candles, and don't feel you have to confine them to their expected holders. Try little glass containers, silver cups, a cluster of votives on a pretty dessert plate or a group of large candles in a shallow wooden bowl. Scatter them around the table or snake them down the center, entwining with ivy or even a favorite scarf.

Chili with Beans

For a different kind of South-of-the-Border Party (page 84), serve bowls of this quick-cooking chili with the salsa, the chicken salad and the cake. If you like, offer chopped onions, grated cheese and chopped cilantro as garnishes.

2	tablespoons olive oil
1 1/2	cups chopped onions
8	large garlic cloves, chopped
3	pounds ground chuck
5	tablespoons chili powder
1	tablespoon ground cumin
1	teaspoon dried basil
1/2	teaspoon dried oregano
1/2	teaspoon dried thyme
1	28-ounce can crushed tomatoes with added puree
1	14 1/2-ounce can low-salt chicken broth
1	12-ounce bottle beer
1	6-ounce can tomato paste
1	15- to 16-ounce can prepared chili beans

• Heat oil in heavy large Dutch oven over medium-high heat. Add onions and garlic. Sauté until onions are translucent, about 8 minutes. Add chuck and sauté until brown, breaking up meat with back of spoon, about 5 minutes. Add chili powder, cumin, basil, oregano and thyme. Stir 2 minutes. Mix in crushed tomatoes, chicken broth, beer and tomato paste. Simmer until thickened to desired consistency, stirring occasionally to prevent sticking, about 1 hour 15 minutes. Mix in beans. Simmer 5 minutes. Season to taste with salt and pepper. *(Can be prepared 3 days ahead. Refrigerate until cold, then cover. Rewarm over low heat before serving.)*

• *6 to 8 servings*

Spiced Lamb and Vegetable Kebabs

If you'd like to grill the main course along with the corn in the Garden Party (page 92), try these delicious kebabs in place of the baked fish. If you serve them with rice, you might not need the bread in the menu.

2	cups plain lowfat yogurt
2	tablespoons fresh lime juice
4	teaspoons minced fresh ginger
1	tablespoon ground cumin
2	garlic cloves, minced
1/2	teaspoon cayenne pepper
3	pounds leg of lamb, cut into 32 large cubes

6	yellow summer squash, cut into 24 1/2-inch-thick pieces
2	red bell peppers, cut into 24 squares
1	red onion, cut into 24 1/2-inch-thick pieces
1/4	cup vegetable oil

• Combine yogurt, lime juice, ginger, cumin, garlic and cayenne in large bowl. Add lamb; stir to coat lamb evenly with yogurt mixture. Marinate at least 20 minutes. *(Can be prepared 1 day ahead. Cover and refrigerate.)*
• Prepare barbecue grill (high heat). Alternate 4 lamb cubes, 3 squash pieces, 3 red pepper squares and 3 onion pieces on each of eight 12-inch-long skewers. Brush meat and vegetables with oil. Grill until meat is cooked to desired doneness, turning and brushing with oil occasionally, about 10 minutes for medium-rare.
• Transfer skewers to platter and serve.
• *8 servings*

Orzo with Lamb, Lima Beans and Feta

This simple lamb stew takes only about 15 minutes to get started, then simmers untended for an hour and a half. Cook up the orzo just before serving—and you have a terrific buffet dish. Serve it with store-bought hummus and pita bread, stuffed grape leaves and sliced cucumbers tossed with yogurt; or, try it in place of the scampi and pilaf in the Dinner and a Movie menu (page 78).

3	tablespoons olive oil
2	onions, chopped
3	large garlic cloves, chopped
2 1/4	pounds lamb stew meat, cut into 3/4-inch pieces
3/4	cup dry white wine
1	28-ounce can peeled tomatoes
1	14 1/2-ounce can peeled tomatoes
1 1/2	10-ounce packages frozen baby lima beans (about 3 cups), thawed
5	tablespoons chopped fresh marjoram or 5 teaspoons dried

1 1/2	pounds orzo (rice-shaped pasta; also called riso)
6	ounces feta cheese, crumbled

• Heat 2 tablespoons oil in heavy large Dutch oven over medium-high heat. Add onions and garlic and cook until tender, stirring frequently, about 10 minutes. Add remaining 1 tablespoon oil. Sprinkle lamb with salt and pepper. Add to Dutch oven and stir until lamb begins to color, about 5 minutes. Add wine and tomatoes with their juices, breaking up tomatoes with spoon. Simmer uncovered until sauce is thick and lamb is tender, about 1 hour 15 minutes. Add lima beans and simmer until just tender, about 15 minutes. Add marjoram and season to taste with salt and pepper. *(Can be prepared 1 day ahead. Cover and refrigerate. Rewarm over medium heat before serving.)*
• Cook orzo in large pot of rapidly boiling salted water until just tender but still firm to bite, stirring occasionally. Drain orzo well. Transfer to large bowl. Spoon lamb stew over. Sprinkle with feta cheese and serve.
• *6 servings*

Spiced Lamb and Vegetable Kebabs (right); Orzo with Lamb, Lima Beans and Feta (far right)

Louisiana Jambalaya

The seafood-rich menu for the Family Reunion (page 64) makes a great meal for fish and shellfish fans, but if there's someone in your family who isn't big on seafood, you might make this jambalaya in place of the fish stew and red rice.

1/2	cup (1 stick) butter
2	red onions, chopped
5	green onions, chopped
1	large green bell pepper, chopped
4	garlic cloves, finely chopped
2	bay leaves
1	jalapeño chili, finely chopped with seeds
1	tablespoon Creole Seasoning*
1/2	teaspoon cayenne pepper
1/2	teaspoon dried oregano
2	tablespoons tomato paste
1	pound andouille sausage** or hot Italian sausage, cut into 1/2-inch pieces
3/4	pound ham, cut into 1/2-inch pieces
2	14 1/2-ounce cans chicken broth
1	16-ounce can plum tomatoes, diced, with liquid
3	cups long-grain rice

• Melt butter in heavy large Dutch oven over medium-high heat. Add red onions, 4 green onions, bell pepper, garlic, bay leaves, jalapeño, Creole Seasoning, cayenne pepper and oregano. Cover and cook until vegetables are tender, stirring occasionally, about 15 minutes. Mix in tomato paste. Add sausage, ham, broth, tomatoes and rice. Bring mixture to simmer. Reduce heat to low, cover and cook until rice is very tender, stirring occasionally, about 1 hour. Garnish with remaining green onion and serve.

*A spice mixture that includes chilies, garlic and other spices. Available at specialty foods stores and also at some supermarkets.

**A smoked pork and beef sausage, available at many specialty foods stores.

• 10 servings

Spareribs with Pineapple-Mustard Glaze

Precooking these ribs reduces the amount of time spent at a hot grill, and none of the meaty flavor is lost because the juices released from the ribs are part of the barbecue glaze. They are an addition to The Cookout menu on page 148; you might also enjoy them at the Picnic in the Country (page 48). (This recipe serves eight when there are burgers on the menu, too, and four when it's the only main course.)

2	pork sparerib racks (about 6 pounds total)
3/4	teaspoon salt
1/2	teaspoon pepper
	Canned low-salt chicken broth
1	12-ounce can frozen pineapple juice concentrate, thawed
1	tablespoon soy sauce
1	tablespoon Dijon mustard
2	teaspoons hot pepper sauce (such as Tabasco)

• Preheat oven to 375°F. Sprinkle ribs with salt and pepper. Wrap each sparerib rack tightly in foil. Arrange ribs on baking sheet and bake until very tender, about 1 hour 20 minutes. Cool ribs in foil 1 hour at room temperature.

• Open foil and pour juices from ribs into bowl. Degrease juices. If necessary, add enough chicken broth to juices to measure 1 1/3 cups liquid. Pour into heavy medium saucepan and boil until mixture is reduced to 1/2 cup, about 10 minutes. Transfer to small bowl. Mix in pineapple concentrate, soy sauce, mustard and hot pepper sauce. (Can be made 1 day ahead. Cover ribs and juices separately and refrigerate.)

• Prepare barbecue (medium heat). Cut ribs into 3-rib sections. Grill until crisp and brown, brushing frequently with pineapple glaze, about 20 minutes.

• 4 to 8 servings

White Bean, Butternut Squash, Kale and Olive Stew

meatless

White Bean, Butternut Squash, Kale and Olive Stew

Make a meatless meal of Dinner in the Kitchen (page 10) by substituting this simple vegetable stew for the chicken and couscous.

1/4	cup olive oil
3	large onions, chopped
6	garlic cloves, minced
1	3 1/4- to 3 1/2-pound butternut squash, peeled, seeded, cut into 1 1/2-inch cubes
3	red bell peppers, seeded, cut into 1 1/2-inch pieces
1 1/2	cups canned vegetable broth
1 1/2	large bunches kale, thick stems trimmed, leaves cut crosswise into 2-inch strips
1	tablespoon dried rubbed sage
5	15-ounce cans cannellini (white kidney beans), rinsed, drained
1	cup brine-cured black olives (such as Kalamata), pitted, halved

Freshly grated Romano cheese

• Heat oil in heavy large Dutch oven over medium-high heat. Add onions and garlic; sauté until tender, about 10 minutes. Add squash; sauté 10 minutes. Add bell peppers and stir to coat with onion mixture. Add broth. Cover and simmer until squash is just tender, about 10 minutes.
• Mix kale and sage into stew. Cover and cook until kale wilts, stirring occasionally, about 8 minutes. Add beans and olives and stir until heated through. Season to taste with salt and pepper.
• Transfer stew to large shallow bowls. Sprinkle generously with cheese.
• *6 servings*

Spiced Vegetable Patties

These delicious potato pancakes, filled with fresh corn, carrot and spinach, would make a fine meatless main course for the Dinner in the Kitchen menu (page 10).

1 1/4	cups fresh corn kernels or frozen, thawed
1	medium carrot, grated
1	medium russet potato, peeled, grated
1/2	medium onion, finely chopped
1/2	cup shredded fresh spinach leaves
6	tablespoons all purpose flour
1/4	cup frozen peas, thawed
1/4	cup finely chopped fresh cilantro
1	jalapeño chili, seeded, minced
2	teaspoons minced garlic
1	teaspoon minced fresh ginger
1	teaspoon ground cumin
1	large egg, beaten to blend
1	tablespoon (or more) vegetable oil
	Plain yogurt
	Purchased Major Grey mango chutney

• Mix first 12 ingredients in large bowl to blend. Season to taste with salt and pepper. Stir in egg. Form 3 tablespoons of mixture into 3-inch-diameter patty. Place on large baking sheet. Repeat with remaining mixture. Refrigerate until firm, about 1 hour.
• Heat 1 tablespoon oil in heavy large nonstick skillet over medium heat. Cook vegetable patties in batches until golden, adding more oil as necessary, about 4 minutes per side. Serve with yogurt and mango chutney.
• *Makes about 12*

Grand Marnier French Toast

Lunch on the Terrace (page 28) could easily become brunch with this lovely dish. Mimosas would get things off to a nice start, and Canadian bacon would be a good accompaniment. If guests linger, you might still have the *pots de crème* for dessert.

4	large eggs
3/4	cup half and half
1/4	cup Grand Marnier or other orange-flavored liqueur or frozen orange juice concentrate, thawed
2	tablespoons sugar
1	tablespoon grated orange peel
1/2	teaspoon vanilla extract
8	3/4-inch-thick French bread slices
4	tablespoons (1/2 stick) butter
	Powdered sugar
	Warm maple syrup

• Whisk first 6 ingredients to blend in medium bowl. Dip each bread slice into egg mixture and arrange in 13 x 9 x 2-inch glass baking dish. Pour remaining egg mixture evenly over bread. Let stand until egg mixture is absorbed, at least 20 minutes. *(Can be prepared 1 day ahead. Cover bread and refrigerate.)*
• Place baking sheet in oven and preheat to 350°F. Melt 2 tablespoons butter in heavy large skillet over medium heat. Add 4 bread slices to skillet and sauté until cooked through and brown, about 3 minutes per side. Place on baking sheet in oven to keep warm. Repeat cooking with remaining 2 tablespoons butter and 4 bread slices. Transfer French toast to 4 plates. Sift powdered sugar over. Serve with maple syrup.
• *4 servings*

Keeping Time

If you think of planning a party in terms of counting down to the event, determining what needs to be done when will be easy. Try sorting the "to-do's" into these five time "zones."

Ahead: Depending on your schedule and where your free time falls, you can do everything from buy the wine to clean the house days ahead of the party. If you're at the store anyway, you could also go ahead and buy the nonperishable items several days in advance. Preparing and freezing dessert or another menu item is also a wise tactic.

One Day Ahead: While you can squeeze the day-ahead chores and the day-of ones into the same day, it's nice to have the luxury of time allowed by going to the grocery the day before the party. You might also make any dishes that can hold a day, and arrange the flowers for the table with any leftover energy.

Day Of: Set the table. Assemble the serving dishes and utensils you'll need. Clean salad greens and refrigerate in the salad spinner or open plastic bags. Cut up crudités and side-dish vegetables (except potatoes, which should be cut just before cooking to prevent blackening) and chill in plastic bags. And of course you'll be popping out to pick up whatever it is that's been forgotten.

Hours Before: Ready the coffee or tea, including cups and saucers. Complete what cooking can be done before the final preparation. Tidy up the house (don't forget the bathrooms), then stop and take a good hour to relax, get yourself ready, have a glass of wine.

At the Party: Greeting guests is your first priority. After everyone has arrived and been outfitted with a drink, you can turn to last-minute cooking and reheating. If you like, encourage everyone to join you in the kitchen, then let the party begin.

pasta

Fettuccine with Shrimp, Scallops and Mussels

This elegant pasta dish mixes fettuccine with seafood and colorful fresh vegetables. It would make a memorable lunch, and so would work nicely in the Lunch on the Terrace menu (page 28).

3 1/2 tablespoons butter
1 1/2 cups fresh white breadcrumbs
   3 tablespoons plus 1 cup chopped fresh basil
   4 teaspoons chopped fresh thyme

   1 pound mussels, scrubbed, debearded
   1 cup water

   3 tablespoons extra-virgin olive oil
   1 zucchini, halved lengthwise, sliced crosswise
   1 yellow summer squash, halved lengthwise, sliced crosswise
   1 red bell pepper, cut into matchstick-size strips
   4 garlic cloves, minced
   8 ounces uncooked large shrimp, peeled, deveined
   8 ounces sea scallops

   1 pound fettuccine

• Melt 1½ tablespoons butter in large nonstick skillet over medium-high heat. Add breadcrumbs; sauté until golden, about 5 minutes. Mix in 3 tablespoons basil and thyme. Remove from heat.

• Combine mussels and 1 cup water in large pot. Cover; boil until mussels open, about 7 minutes (discard any mussels that do not open). Using tongs, transfer mussels to bowl. Tent with foil. Strain cooking liquid into small bowl.

• Heat 1 tablespoon oil in large nonstick skillet over medium-high heat. Add zucchini, squash and red pepper and sauté until crisp-tender, about 5 minutes. Transfer to bowl. Melt 2 tablespoons butter with 2 tablespoons oil in same skillet. Add garlic; sauté 30 seconds. Add shrimp, scallops and ½ cup basil and sauté 3 minutes. Add mussel cooking liquid; simmer until shellfish are cooked through, about 3 minutes. Add vegetables; stir to heat through.

• Meanwhile, cook pasta in large pot of boiling salted water until just tender but still firm to bite. Drain.

• Pour vegetables and shellfish over pasta; toss to coat. Season with salt and pepper. Sprinkle with ½ cup basil. Top with mussels and breadcrumbs.

• *4 servings*

Penne with Sausage, Peas and Mascarpone

Subtle and strong flavors work together in this terrific dish—among them spicy Italian sausage and rich, creamy mascarpone cheese. It comes together quickly, and would work in place of the rigatoni in the Pasta Party (page 34).

3/4	pound hot Italian sausages, casings removed
3/4	pound sweet Italian sausages, casings removed
1	cup chopped onion
1 1/4	cups whipping cream
3/4	cup canned low-salt chicken broth
1	pound penne
2	cups frozen peas
2/3	cup mascarpone cheese*
3/4	cup freshly grated Parmesan cheese

• Sauté sausages in Dutch oven over high heat until brown, breaking into small pieces with back of spoon, about 12 minutes. Using slotted spoon, transfer sausage to bowl. Pour off all but 1 tablespoon drippings. Add onion and sauté until light brown, about 6 minutes. Add cream; boil 5 minutes. Add broth; boil until reduced to sauce consistency, stirring occasionally, about 8 minutes. Return sausage to pot.

• Cook penne in large pot of boiling salted water until pasta is just tender but still firm to bite.

• Meanwhile, bring sauce to simmer over medium heat. Add peas and mascarpone and simmer until peas are tender, about 6 minutes.

• Drain pasta. Add to sauce; toss to coat. Mix in Parmesan. Season with salt and pepper. Transfer to large bowl.

Italian cream cheese available at Italian markets and some supermarkets. If mascarpone is unavailable, mix 6 tablespoons cream cheese with 5 tablespoons whipping cream.

• *6 servings*

Fettuccine with Shrimp, Scallops and Mussels (far left); Penne with Sausage, Peas and Mascarpone (left)

Linguine with Chicken, Garlic and Basil

This attractive pasta dish could replace the chicken salad in the Lunch on the Terrace menu (page 28).

1/4	cup plus 1 tablespoon (about) olive oil
1/4	cup minced garlic
3/4	pound linguine
1 1/2	pounds skinless boneless chicken breasts, cut into thin strips
2	poblano chilies,* seeded, cut into matchstick-size strips
3	plum tomatoes, seeded, diced
1/2	cup thinly sliced fresh basil
4	ounces prosciutto, chopped
2	tablespoons (1/4 stick) butter
1	cup freshly grated Parmesan cheese

• Heat ¼ cup oil in heavy small skillet over medium heat. Add garlic and sauté until light golden brown, about 6 minutes. Strain oil into glass measuring cup; reserve garlic. Add enough oil to measuring cup to measure ¼ cup. Set aside.

• Cook linguine in large pot of boiling salted water until tender but still firm to bite, stirring occasionally.

• Meanwhile, heat reserved oil in heavy large skillet over medium-high heat. Add chicken and sauté 5 minutes. Add poblanos and sauté 2 minutes. Add tomatoes, ¼ cup basil, prosciutto and 2 tablespoons cooked garlic and sauté until chicken is cooked through, about 1 minute. Remove from heat. Add butter and stir just until melted.

• Drain linguine and place in large bowl. Add chicken mixture and ½ cup Parmesan; toss to coat. Season with salt and pepper. Sprinkle with remaining ¼ cup basil and 2 tablespoons cooked garlic. Serve with remaining Parmesan.

*A fresh green chili, often called a pasilla, available at Latin American markets and some supermarkets.

• 4 servings

Linguine with Chicken, Garlic and Basil (far left); Spinach and Cheese-stuffed Pasta Shells (left)

Spinach and Cheese-stuffed Pasta Shells

This easy and stylish meatless pasta dish could replace either the fettuccine or the rigatoni in the Pasta Party menu (page 34).

- 2   10-ounce packages frozen chopped spinach, thawed
- 1   15-ounce container ricotta cheese
- 1   cup (about 4 ounces) freshly grated Parmesan cheese
- 2   tablespoons fennel seeds
- 2   tablespoons chopped fresh basil or 2 teaspoons dried
- 3   garlic cloves, minced

- 3 1/2   cups purchased marinara or spaghetti sauce
- 32   jumbo pasta shells, freshly cooked
   Additional grated Parmesan cheese

- Squeeze spinach dry. Transfer spinach to large bowl. Add ricotta, ½ cup Parmesan, fennel, basil and garlic to bowl. Season mixture with salt and pepper; blend thoroughly.
- Preheat oven to 350°F. Spoon ½ cup marinara sauce evenly over bottom of 9 x 13 x 2-inch baking dish. Fill each pasta shell with spinach mixture. Place shells, filling side up, in dish. Spoon remaining sauce over shells. Sprinkle with ½ cup Parmesan. Cover loosely with foil and bake until heated through, about 30 minutes. Serve, passing additional Parmesan separately.

- *6 servings*

Spaghettini with Spicy Tomato Sauce

The wonderful sauce here combines tomatoes, red wine and Italian sausage with a mix of fresh vegetables for an updated spaghetti sauce. It can be made a day ahead and tossed with the pasta just before serving. Try this entrée in place of the scampi in the Dinner and a Movie menu (page 78).

- 2   tablespoons olive oil
- 1   carrot, grated
- 1   red bell pepper, seeded, chopped
- 1/2   onion, chopped
- 4   garlic cloves, chopped
- 1   28-ounce can crushed tomatoes with added puree
- 1   14 1/2-ounce can Italian-style stewed tomatoes
- 1/2   cup dry red wine
- 1 1/4   teaspoons (or more) dried crushed red pepper
- 2   teaspoons dried oregano
- 1/2   pound hot Italian sausage, casings removed

- 4   ounces mushrooms, sliced
- 2   zucchini, chopped
   Generous pinch of sugar
   Dash of balsamic vinegar

- 1 1/2   pounds spaghettini or other pasta
   Chopped fresh parsley
   Freshly grated Parmesan cheese

- Heat oil in heavy large saucepan over medium heat. Add carrot, bell pepper, onion and garlic and sauté until tender, about 10 minutes. Add crushed tomatoes with puree, stewed tomatoes with juices, wine, dried red pepper and oregano. Bring to simmer. Cook sausage in heavy medium skillet over medium-high heat until cooked through, breaking up with back of spoon, about 5 minutes. Using slotted spoon, transfer sausage to sauce. Reserve drippings in skillet. Cover sauce partially and simmer 1½ hours, stirring occasionally.
- Add mushrooms and zucchini to skillet with drippings; sauté over medium-high heat until tender, about 5 minutes. Stir into sauce. Simmer uncovered until sauce is thick, about 20 minutes. Add sugar and vinegar. Season with salt, pepper and more dried red pepper, if desired. *(Can be made 1 day ahead. Cover; chill. Bring to simmer before using.)*
- Cook pasta in large pot of boiling salted water until tender but still firm to bite, stirring occasionally. Drain. Transfer pasta to large bowl. Toss pasta with enough sauce to coat. Sprinkle with chopped parsley. Serve, passing grated Parmesan and remaining sauce separately.

- *6 servings*

the cookout

Menu for Eight

- Tomato Salad with Basil-Buttermilk Dressing (page 120)

- Grilled Hamburgers with Sour Cream and Herbs (page 138)

- Three-Pepper Ketchup (page 139)

- Spareribs with Pineapple-Mustard Glaze (page 142)

- Grilled Red Onions (page 121)

- Hot and Smoky Baked Beans (page 122)

- Coleslaw

- Watermelon

- Lemonade, Iced Tea and Beer

- Ice Cream and Cookies

149

All it takes is one warm spring weekend, and the urge to uncover the barbecue, clean it up and get cooking takes over. It's a fever, one that doesn't subside until the last days of fall — and it's a great excuse for a party. ★ A cookout is easy, by nature: It's relaxed and casual — both the mood and the food. And it lends itself to occasions of many kinds, from a Father's Day feast to a neighborly get-together, a Fourth of July celebration to an afternoon pool party. Nothing fancy required; shorts a given. ★ The only trick is timing: Nobody wants to be tending the grill all day, worrying about when the food will be done. This menu eliminates the guesswork. The spareribs are prebaked, needing only basting and crisping over the fire before serving. The hamburgers, made extra moist by the addition of sour cream, are your basic delicious barbecue fare, with grilled onions and a chunky jalapeño-spiked ketchup upping the ante. Add a pot of homemade baked beans and a large platter of sliced tomatoes with buttermilk-basil dressing, and the meal becomes memorable. ★ Simplify preparations by purchasing other menu items: good-quality buns for the burgers, deli coleslaw, watermelon, ice cream (with cones and sprinkles for the kids) and cookies. After all, it's not just the cooking that should be outdoors, but the cook as well.

mix- and- match desserts

pies and tarts

Peach Tart with Almond Crust

Another fitting ending to the Garden Party menu (page 92).

CRUST

1	cup sliced almonds (about 4 ounces)
1	cup all purpose flour
1/2	cup sugar
1/2	cup chilled unsalted butter, cut into pieces
1	egg yolk, beaten to blend
1/2	teaspoon vanilla extract

FILLING

2	tablespoons peach preserves
1/4	cup sliced almonds, finely chopped
1 1/2	pounds ripe peaches, peeled, pitted, cut into 1/2-inch-thick slices
3	tablespoons sugar
1 1/2	teaspoons grated lemon peel
2	tablespoons (1/4 stick) unsalted butter
	Additional sliced almonds
	Vanilla ice cream or mascarpone cheese

• FOR CRUST: Butter 9-inch-diameter tart pan with removable bottom. Coarsely grind almonds in processor. Add flour and sugar and continue processing until nuts are finely ground. Add butter and process using on/off turns until mixture resembles coarse meal. Pour egg yolk and vanilla over flour mixture and process using on/off turns until mixture forms large moist clumps. Press enough dough onto bottom and up sides of tart pan to form ¼-inch-thick crust. (Reserve any remaining dough for another use.) Refrigerate crust until well chilled, about 30 minutes. (*Can be prepared 1 day ahead. Cover tightly with plastic wrap and refrigerate.*)

• Preheat oven to 375°F. Bake crust until golden brown, about 20 minutes. Cool on rack. Maintain oven temperature.

• FOR FILLING: Spread preserves evenly over bottom of crust. Sprinkle ¼ cup almonds over preserves. Arrange sliced peaches atop almonds in slightly overlapping spiral pattern. Sprinkle peaches with sugar and lemon peel. Dot top of tart with butter. Sprinkle with additional almonds. Bake until peaches are tender, about 35 minutes. Cool slightly. Serve warm or at room temperature with vanilla ice cream or mascarpone cheese.

• *8 servings*

Summer Fruit Shortcake Pie

This version of the classic American dessert isn't limited to berries alone. The shortcake-like crust is great with all fruits. Use whatever's in season and serve it at the Garden Party (page 92).

CRUST

1	cup all purpose flour
1/4	cup pecans, toasted
3	tablespoons firmly packed light brown sugar
1 1/2	teaspoons baking powder
1/4	teaspoon salt
1/4	cup plus 1 tablespoon chilled unsalted butter
2	tablespoons milk

FILLING

1/2	cup sugar
2	tablespoons cornstarch
	Pinch of salt
1/2	cup plus 2 tablespoons fresh orange juice
2	tablespoons fresh lemon juice
1/4	cup Grand Marnier or other orange liqueur
6	cups mixed fruit, such as hulled strawberries, raspberries, sliced bananas, sliced pitted plums, blueberries, and cantaloupe or honeydew melon balls
	Whipped cream or vanilla ice cream (optional)

• FOR CRUST: Preheat oven to 425°F. Combine first 5 ingredients in processor and process until pecans are finely ground. Add butter and process using on/off turns until mixture resembles coarse meal. Add milk and pulse until large moist clumps form. Gather dough into ball. Knead dough on lightly floured surface until smooth. Roll dough out between 2 sheets of plastic wrap to 11-inch round. Remove top sheet of plastic. Invert dough into 9-inch-diameter pie pan. Remove plastic wrap. Crimp dough edges to make decorative border. Bake until crust is golden, about 14 minutes. Cool completely. (*Crust can be prepared up to 6 hours ahead.*)

• FOR FILLING: Combine sugar, cornstarch and pinch of salt in heavy large saucepan. Gradually mix in orange juice and lemon juice. Stir constantly over medium heat until mixture thickens and boils 1 minute. Remove from heat and stir in Grand Marnier liqueur. Cool filling 10 minutes.

• Place fruit in large bowl. Pour orange juice mixture over. Toss well to coat. Spoon fruit into crust, mounding in center. Refrigerate pie until fruit is set, about 30 minutes. (*Can be prepared 3 hours ahead.*) Serve with whipped cream or vanilla ice cream if desired.

• *8 servings*

Peach Tart with Almond Crust

Just a Reminder

Ever leave the chopped parsley in its dish in the refrigerator? How about the bread in the oven? It happens to even the most organized party giver. To help, here's a list of some of the things that are most likely to be forgotten.

Extra hangers for the coat closet.

Hand towels in the bathrooms.

A large cooler, to hold the beer, soda and wine that won't fit in the refrigerator.

Extra ice.

Extra lemons and limes, to garnish mineral water as well as cocktails.

Coasters.

Cocktail napkins.

Candles.

Salt and pepper for the table.

A sugar bowl and creamer (with cream in it!) to set out with coffee.

Coffee spoons.

Decaffeinated coffee.

Good-quality loose tea and a teapot (for those who prefer tea).

Coconut-Almond Chocolate Tart

If Cocktails at Five (page 18) crosses the dinner hour and you'd like to offer a little something sweet before your guests leave, try this decadent chocolate tart, which combines the luscious flavors of a popular candy bar. A little slice goes a long way.

CRUST
1 1/2	cups toasted almonds
1/4	cup lightly packed golden brown sugar
1/4	cup (1/2 stick) unsalted butter, melted

FILLING
1/2	cup canned coconut cream (such as Coco Lopez)
3	ounces imported white chocolate (such as Lindt), chopped
1/4	cup sour cream
1/4	cup (1/2 stick) unsalted butter, cut into pieces, room temperature
1 1/4	cups lightly packed shredded sweetened coconut

TOPPING
1/4	cup whipping cream
3	tablespoons unsalted butter
2	tablespoons light corn syrup
4	ounces bittersweet (not unsweetened) chocolate, chopped
2	ounces imported white chocolate (such as Lindt), chopped, melted
26	(about) whole almonds, toasted

• FOR CRUST: Preheat oven to 350°F. Coarsely chop almonds in processor. Add sugar and butter and process using on/off turns until finely chopped. Using plastic wrap as aid, press mixture firmly into bottom and up sides of 9-inch-diameter tart pan with removable bottom. Bake 10 minutes. Cool on rack.

• FOR FILLING: Bring coconut cream to simmer in heavy small saucepan. Reduce heat to low. Add white chocolate and stir until melted. Pour into medium bowl. Whisk in sour cream. Add butter and whisk until butter melts and mixture is smooth. Stir in coconut. Chill until filling is very cold but not set, about 1 hour. Spoon filling into crust; smooth top. Refrigerate until set.

• FOR TOPPING: Bring first 3 ingredients to simmer in heavy small saucepan, stirring frequently. Reduce heat to low. Add bittersweet chocolate and stir until melted. Reserve 3 tablespoons hot topping. Pour remainder over tart, covering filling. Spread topping with back of spoon to cover filling evenly.

• Quickly spoon melted white chocolate into parchment cone. Pipe white chocolate in parallel vertical lines over topping, spacing evenly. To form decorative pattern, draw tip of small knife from left to right through white chocolate lines. Draw knife from right to left through white chocolate lines. Repeat, spacing evenly and alternating direction knife is moved. Dip round end of 1 almond halfway into reserved chocolate topping. Place sideways at edge of tart. Repeat with remaining almonds, arranging side by side around tart. Chill overnight. (Can be prepared 5 days ahead.) Remove pan sides. Cut into wedges.

• *12 servings*

Coconut-Almond
Chocolate Tart

Tropical Lime Mousse Pie

This do-ahead dessert is perfect after a barbecue—like the one on page 56.

CRUST
8	whole graham crackers
1/2	cup sweetened flaked coconut
7	tablespoons butter, melted

FILLING
1/4	cup amber (gold) rum
1 1/2	teaspoons unflavored gelatin
4	large eggs
1	cup sugar
2/3	cup fresh lime juice
3	tablespoons grated lime peel
1	cup chilled whipping cream

Sweetened flaked coconut, toasted

• FOR CRUST: Preheat oven to 350°F. Process graham crackers in processor until finely ground. Add coconut and butter and pulse to blend. Press crumb mixture on bottom and 1¾ inches up sides of 8-inch-diameter springform pan. Bake until golden brown on edges, about 10 minutes. Cool completely.

• FOR FILLING: Place rum in small bowl. Sprinkle gelatin over. Let stand 10 minutes to soften. Whisk eggs, sugar and lime juice in heavy small saucepan over medium-high heat until mixture thickens and just comes to boil, about 4 minutes. Remove from heat. Add gelatin mixture and stir until gelatin melts. Mix in 2 tablespoons grated lime peel. Refrigerate lime mixture until cold but not set, stirring occasionally, about 30 minutes.

• Whip chilled cream until soft peaks form. Fold whipped cream into lime mixture. Pour filling into crust. Refrigerate until filling is set, about 3 hours. *(Can be prepared up to 1 day ahead.)*

• Sprinkle pie with toasted coconut and remaining 1 tablespoon lime peel. Cut into wedges and serve.

• *8 servings*

Fresh Fig Tart

This luscious combination of creamy custard and ripe fresh figs in a short, buttery crust would be a fitting ending to either the Picnic in the Country (page 48) or the Garden Party (page 92).

CRUST
10	tablespoons (1 1/4 sticks) unsalted butter, room temperature
1/3	cup plus 1 1/2 tablespoons sugar
1	egg yolk
1	teaspoon vanilla extract
1 3/4	cups all purpose flour

FILLING
1 1/2	cups half and half
1 1/2	tablespoons honey
1	vanilla bean, split lengthwise
7	tablespoons sugar
3	tablespoons plus 1 teaspoon cornstarch
1	large egg
1	large egg yolk
3	pints fresh ripe figs

• FOR CRUST: Using electric mixer, beat butter and sugar in large bowl until fluffy. Mix in egg yolk and vanilla. Add flour and mix until well combined. Shape dough into ball and flatten into disk. Wrap in plastic and refrigerate 30 minutes. *(Can be prepared 1 day ahead. Soften slightly before rolling out.)*

• FOR FILLING: Combine half and half and honey in heavy medium saucepan; scrape in seeds from vanilla bean; add bean. Bring to simmer over medium-high heat. Remove from heat; remove bean. Whisk sugar, cornstarch, egg and egg yolk in medium bowl. Gradually whisk in hot half and half mixture. Return mixture to pan and whisk over medium heat until custard boils and thickens, about 3 minutes. Transfer to bowl. Refrigerate until cooled to room temperature, whisking occasionally. *(Can be prepared 1 day ahead. Cover with plastic wrap and refrigerate.)*

• Position rack in center of oven and preheat to 350°F. Lightly butter 9-inch-diameter tart pan with removable bottom. Roll out dough on lightly floured surface to 13-inch round. Transfer to prepared pan. Trim edges. Pierce bottom of crust lightly with fork. Chill 20 minutes. Bake until light golden, about 25 minutes. Transfer to rack; cool completely.

• Cut enough figs into small wedges to measure 1 generous cup. Fold fig pieces into filling. Spread filling evenly in prepared crust. Cut remaining figs in half lengthwise. Arrange fig halves in concentric circles atop filling, pointed ends toward center, covering filling completely. Refrigerate at least 1 hour and up to 3 hours. Cut tart into wedges.

• *8 servings*

Tropical Lime Mousse Pie

Fresh Fig Tart

Tarte Tatin

This caramel apple-topped pastry is *the* classic bistro dessert. Here's a simple recipe to try if you've always wanted to make this irresistible sweet. Serve it at the Bistro Supper (page 42), of course.

SOUR CREAM PASTRY

1 1/2	cups all purpose flour
2	tablespoons sugar
1/2	teaspoon salt
3/4	cup (1 1/2 sticks) chilled unsalted butter, cut into 3/4-inch pieces
6	tablespoons chilled sour cream

APPLE FILLING

1/2	cup (1 stick) plus 1 tablespoon unsalted butter, room temperature
1 1/2	cups sugar
11	medium-size Pippin apples (about 4 3/4 pounds), peeled, quartered, cored
1	egg, beaten to blend (glaze)

Crème fraîche or sour cream

• FOR PASTRY: Blend flour, sugar and salt in large bowl of heavy-duty mixer fitted with whisk attachment. Add butter and beat at medium-low speed until butter is size of small lima beans, about 3 minutes. Add sour cream and beat until moist clumps form, about 1 minute. Gather dough into smooth ball; flatten into 6-inch-diameter disk. Wrap dough in plastic; refrigerate until cold, at least 2 hours. (*Can be made 1 day ahead. Keep refrigerated. Let soften slightly before rolling out.*)

• FOR FILLING: Spread butter over bottom of 12-inch-diameter ovenproof nonstick skillet with sloping sides (skillet should be at least 1¾ inches deep). Reserve 2 tablespoons sugar; sprinkle remaining sugar over butter. Place skillet over medium-low heat and cook until butter melts, sugar begins to dissolve and mixture starts to bubble, about 3 minutes.

• Remove from heat. Arrange apples on their sides around edge of skillet, placing tightly together. Arrange as many of remaining apples as will fit, pointed ends up, in 2 circles in center of skillet. Sprinkle with 2 tablespoons sugar.

• Set skillet over medium-high heat; boil until thick peanut butter-color syrup forms, repositioning skillet often for even cooking and adding remaining apples as space permits, about 45 minutes (syrup will continue to darken during baking). Remove from heat; wrap handle several times with heavy-duty foil.

• Meanwhile, position rack in center of oven and preheat to 425°F.

• Roll out pastry on floured surface to 12-inch round; place over apples. Cut four 2-inch slits in top of pastry. Press pastry down around apples at edge of skillet; brush pastry with some of egg glaze.

• Bake tart until pastry is deep golden brown, about 30 minutes. Transfer to work surface; cool 1 minute. Cut around edge of skillet to loosen pastry. Place large platter over skillet. Using oven mitts as aid, hold skillet and platter together and invert, allowing tart to fall onto platter. Carefully lift off skillet. Rearrange any apples that may have become dislodged. Cool tart for 30 minutes.

• Cut warm tart into wedges. Serve with crème fraîche or sour cream.

• *10 to 12 servings*

Tarte Tatin

Milk Chocolate-Pecan Tartlets

Make these terrific little tartlets the day before and add them to the spread for The Dessert Buffet (page 168). Or, have them after cocktails and hors d'oeuvres (page 18).

CRUST

1 1/4	cups all purpose flour
1/3	cup pecans, toasted
1/4	cup sugar
	Pinch of salt
6	tablespoons (3/4 stick) chilled unsalted butter, cut into pieces
1	large egg yolk
1 1/2	teaspoons (or more) whipping cream

Nonstick vegetable oil spray

FILLING

9	ounces imported milk chocolate (such as Lindt), finely chopped
1/3	cup plus 1 tablespoon whipping cream
3	tablespoons finely chopped toasted pecans
1/4	cup (about) apricot preserves
	Pecan halves
	Grated milk chocolate

• FOR CRUST: Blend first 4 ingredients in processor until nuts are finely chopped. Using on/off turns, add butter; process until mixture resembles coarse meal. Mix yolk and 1 1/2 teaspoons cream in bowl. Add to flour mixture; process until moist clumps form. If dough is dry, add more cream by teaspoonfuls to moisten. Gather dough into ball. Flatten into disk. Wrap in plastic; chill 4 hours.

• Preheat oven to 350°F. Spray eighteen 3-inch tartlet pans with oil spray. Press 1 tablespoon dough onto bottom and up sides of each pan. Arrange tartlet pans on heavy large baking sheet. Bake until crusts are golden, piercing with fork if bubbles form, about 10 minutes. Transfer pans to rack; cool completely.

• FOR FILLING: Melt 9 ounces chocolate in top of double boiler over simmering water, stirring often. Remove from heat. Bring cream just to simmer in small saucepan. Pour hot cream into chocolate; stir until very smooth. Stir in chopped pecans. Transfer filling to small bowl. Cover; chill until filling is consistency of thick pudding, about 2 hours.

• Using small knife, loosen crusts from pans. Turn crusts out. Spread 1 teaspoon preserves in each crust. Spoon 1 tablespoon filling over. Garnish with nut halves and grated chocolate. Chill until filling is firm, about 1 hour. (*Can be made 1 day ahead. Cover; chill.*) Serve cold.

• *Makes 18*

cakes

Espresso and Chocolate Swirl Cheesecake

End an already elegant picnic (page 48) with this equally elegant dessert, which lends itself to being made ahead (up to three days) and packed to carry (a sturdy plastic container will do).

CRUST

1	9-ounce package chocolate wafer cookies
6	tablespoons (3/4 stick) unsalted butter, melted, cooled

FILLING

2	tablespoons instant espresso powder
1	tablespoon water
3	8-ounce packages cream cheese, room temperature
1	cup sugar
3	large eggs
1/4	cup (1/2 stick) unsalted butter, melted, cooled
1	tablespoon finely ground coffee
6	ounces bittersweet (not unsweetened) or semisweet chocolate, chopped
1/4	cup whipping cream

• FOR CRUST: Position rack in center of oven and preheat to 400°F. Grind cookies in processor. Add butter and process using on/off turns until crumbs are moist. Press crumbs on bottom and 1 1/2 inches up sides of 9-inch-diameter springform pan with 2 3/4-inch-high sides. Wrap outside of pan with aluminum foil.

• FOR FILLING: In small bowl, dissolve instant espresso in 1 tablespoon water. Using electric mixer, beat cream cheese in large bowl until smooth. Add sugar and continue beating until mixture is light and fluffy. Add eggs 1 at a time, beating well after each addition. Mix in espresso mixture, butter and coffee .

• Combine chocolate and cream in heavy small saucepan. Stir over low heat until chocolate melts. Pour half of cheese filling (about 2 1/2 cups) into prepared crust. Drop 5 tablespoons melted chocolate mixture by tablespoons around edge of filling, spacing evenly. Use small sharp knife to swirl chocolate into filling. Carefully pour remaining cheese filling over. Drop remaining chocolate mixture by tablespoons into center 6 inches of filling, spacing evenly. Swirl mixtures together using tip of knife.

• Bake cheesecake until edges are puffed and beginning to crack and top is golden brown, about 40 minutes (center will not be set). Cool on rack. Chill overnight. (*Can be prepared 3 days ahead.*)

• Run small sharp knife around edge of pan to loosen cheesecake. Release pan sides. Let stand at room temperature 30 minutes. Transfer to platter and serve.

• *10 servings*

Mandarin Chocolate Cake

This big, beautiful chocolate cake makes a big impression at the end of The Potluck menu on page 126, but it would make a festive occasion of any number of events, from the Bistro Supper (page 42) to the Family Reunion (page 64).

CAKE

12	ounces semisweet chocolate, chopped
3/4	cup (1 1/2 sticks) unsalted butter, cut into 8 pieces, room temperature
1	cup sugar
1 1/2	tablespoons grated orange peel
4	large eggs
1	large egg yolk
3/4	cup cake flour
1/4	teaspoon (generous) ground ginger
1	cup chopped toasted almonds
3/4	cup minced crystallized ginger

GLAZE

1/2	cup whipping cream
2	tablespoons plus 2 teaspoons Grand Marnier
11	ounces semisweet chocolate, minced

4	oranges, thinly sliced

• FOR CAKE: Preheat oven to 350°F. Butter 10-inch-diameter cake pan. Line bottom with parchment; butter paper. Dust pan with flour. Melt semisweet chocolate in top of double boiler over simmering water. Remove from over water. Add unsalted butter 1 tablespoon at a time, mixing until melted and smooth. Mix in sugar and grated orange peel. Mix in eggs 1 at a time. Stir in egg yolk. Add cake flour and ground ginger, then chopped toasted almonds and crystallized ginger and stir to combine. Transfer batter to prepared pan. Bake until just springy to touch, about 1 hour 5 minutes. Cool cake in pan on rack 15 minutes. Turn out onto rack, remove paper and cool.

• FOR GLAZE: Scald whipping cream with Grand Marnier in heavy small saucepan. Remove from heat. Add chocolate and mix until smooth. Cool glaze until thick enough to spread.

• Arrange cake flat side up on rack. Spread glaze evenly over top and sides of cake. Refrigerate until glaze is firm, about 30 minutes. Transfer cake to serving platter. *(Cake can be prepared 1 day ahead. Cover and refrigerate. Bring to room temperature.)*

• Cut orange slices in half. Twist three and place in center of cake. Arrange remaining orange slices around edge of platter and serve.

• *12 servings*

Mandarin Chocolate Cake

Banana "Turtle" Torte

Bananas and the chocolate-caramel-pecan combination of the classic turtle candy come together in this superb dessert, which has the texture of a chewy brownie. Kids will love it, making the cake a good choice for the Family Reunion (page 64).

CARAMEL

1 1/2	cups sugar
1/2	cup water
3/4	cup whipping cream
6	tablespoons (3/4 stick) unsalted butter, room temperature
	Pinch of salt

CAKE

6	ounces unsweetened chocolate, chopped
1/2	cup (1 stick) unsalted butter
4	eggs
2	cups sugar
1	cup all purpose flour
1	teaspoon vanilla extract
1/4	teaspoon salt
2 1/4	cups coarsely chopped pecans (about 9 1/2 ounces)

1 1/2	cups chilled whipping cream
2	tablespoons banana liqueur (optional)
4	bananas, thinly sliced (about 2 pounds)
	Additional coarsely chopped pecans (optional)

• FOR CARAMEL: Combine sugar and water in heavy medium saucepan; stir over low heat until sugar dissolves. Increase heat and bring to boil. Cook without stirring until caramel is deep amber color, brushing down any crystals that form on sides of pan with wet pastry brush and swirling occasionally, about 10 minutes. Remove from heat; carefully add cream. (Mixture will bubble vigorously.) Return to low heat and whisk until smooth. Add butter and salt and whisk until smooth. Cool to room temperature. *(Can be made 3 days ahead. Cover and chill. Before using, warm over low heat until just pourable.)*

• FOR CAKE: Preheat oven to 350°F. Butter three 9-inch-diameter cake pans with 1 1/2-inch-high sides. Line bottoms of pans with parchment or waxed paper; butter paper. Combine chocolate and butter in heavy large saucepan. Stir over low heat until melted. Cool. Whisk in eggs and sugar. Stir in flour, vanilla and salt. Divide batter among prepared pans and spread evenly. Sprinkle 3/4 cup pecans atop each. Bake cakes until set and tester inserted into center comes out with a few moist crumbs still attached, about 15 minutes. Cool in pans on rack. Turn out layers and remove waxed paper. *(Can be made 1 day ahead. Store airtight.)*

• Beat whipping cream and liqueur to stiff peaks. Place 1 cake layer pecan side up on platter. Drizzle 1/4 cup caramel over. Cover with layer of bananas. Spread 1 cup whipped cream over bananas. Drizzle 3 tablespoons caramel over cream. Top with second cake layer. Repeat layering with 1/4 cup caramel, bananas, 1 cup whipped cream and 3 tablespoons caramel. Top with remaining cake layer. Drizzle 1/4 cup caramel over cake. Transfer remaining whipped cream to pastry bag fitted with large star tip. Pipe rosettes of cream around top edge of torte. Garnish with bananas. Sprinkle with pecans. *(Can be made 4 hours ahead. Refrigerate.)* Rewarm remaining caramel. Serve torte with caramel.

• *10 to 12 servings*

Pound Cake with Strawberry Sauce and Chantilly Cream

A simple, fresh-tasting dessert that turns purchased pound cake into something really wonderful. It would make a nice ending to the Lunch on the Terrace (page 28) or the Back-Yard Barbecue (page 56). And it's a natural in The Brunch menu on page 112.

3	cups hulled fresh strawberries
6	tablespoons crème de cassis
4	tablespoons sugar

1	cup chilled whipping cream
1	teaspoon vanilla extract

1	12-ounce pound cake, cut into 1/2-inch-thick slices
2	1-pint baskets strawberries, hulled, sliced

• Puree 3 cups berries with cassis and 2 tablespoons sugar in processor. Strain through sieve to remove seeds. Cover and refrigerate until well chilled. *(Strawberry sauce can be prepared 1 day ahead.)*

• Using electric mixer, whip cream with remaining 2 tablespoons sugar and vanilla in large bowl to soft peaks. *(Whipped cream can be prepared 4 hours ahead. Cover and chill.)*

• Arrange pound cake slices on plates. Top cake with sliced berries. Spoon strawberry sauce over. Top with whipped cream and serve.

• *8 servings*

Triple-Layer Devil's Food Cake

Here's a chocolate cake that's as all-American as the Back-Yard Barbecue (page 56), and an impressive ending to that festive menu.

CAKE

1 3/4 cups water
1 tablespoon instant espresso powder or instant coffee powder
1 cup unsweetened cocoa powder

2 1/4 cups sifted all purpose flour
1 1/2 teaspoons baking powder
3/4 teaspoon baking soda
1/2 teaspoon salt
1 cup (2 sticks) unsalted butter, room temperature
2 cups firmly packed dark brown sugar (about 1 pound)
2 large eggs
2 large egg yolks

FROSTING

2 vanilla beans, split lengthwise
1 1/4 cups whipping cream
1/2 cup sugar
4 large egg yolks
1/8 teaspoon salt
1 pound bittersweet (not unsweetened) or semisweet chocolate, finely chopped
3/4 cup (1 1/2 sticks) unsalted butter, cut into pieces, room temperature
1/2 cup light corn syrup
1/4 cup sour cream

White and milk chocolate shavings

• FOR CAKE: Preheat oven to 350°F. Lightly butter three 9-inch cake pans with 1¾-inch-high sides. Line pan bottoms with waxed paper rounds. Butter waxed paper.

Triple-Layer Devil's Food Cake (top left); Chocolate Zucchini Cake (bottom left)

• Bring water and coffee powder to boil in heavy small saucepan. Remove from heat. Add cocoa and whisk until smooth. Cool completely.
• Sift flour, baking powder, baking soda and salt into medium bowl. Using electric mixer, beat butter in large bowl until fluffy. Add sugar in 4 additions, beating well after each addition and scraping down sides of bowl occasionally. Add eggs and yolks 1 at a time, beating just to blend after each addition. Using rubber spatula, mix dry ingredients into butter mixture alternately with cocoa mixture, beginning and ending with dry ingredients. Divide batter evenly among prepared pans. Bake until toothpick inserted into centers comes out clean, about 23 minutes. Cool cakes in pans on racks 10 minutes. Turn out onto racks. Peel off waxed paper; cool completely. *(Can be prepared 1 day ahead. Return cakes to pans and cover tightly with foil. Let stand at room temperature.)*
• FOR FROSTING: Carefully scrape seeds from vanilla beans into heavy large saucepan (save beans for another use). Add cream, sugar, yolks and salt and blend well. Stir over medium-low heat until custard thickens and leaves path on back of spoon when finger is drawn across, about 7 minutes; do not boil. Mix in chocolate, butter and corn syrup. Remove from heat; stir until smooth. Mix in sour cream. Transfer frosting to bowl and refrigerate until spreadable, stirring occasionally, about 1 hour.
• Place 1 cake layer on platter. Spread 1 cup frosting over. Repeat with second cake layer and frosting. Top with third cake layer. Spread remaining frosting over top and sides of cake, swirling decoratively. *(Can be made 1 day ahead. Cover with cake dome and chill. Let stand at room temperature 1 hour before serving.)*
• Sprinkle white and milk chocolate shavings thickly over top of cake.
• *12 servings*

Chocolate Zucchini Cake

A sly way to slip the children some vegetables, and a delicious way to end the Family Reunion (page 64).

2 1/4	cups sifted all purpose flour
1/2	cup unsweetened cocoa powder
1	teaspoon baking soda
1	teaspoon salt
1 3/4	cups sugar
1/2	cup (1 stick) unsalted butter, room temperature
1/2	cup vegetable oil
2	large eggs
1	teaspoon vanilla extract
1/2	cup buttermilk
2	cups grated unpeeled zucchini (about 2 1/2 medium)
1	6-ounce package (about 1 cup) semisweet chocolate chips
3/4	cup chopped walnuts

• Preheat oven to 325°F. Butter and flour 13 x 9 x 2-inch baking pan. Sift flour, cocoa powder, baking soda and salt into medium bowl. Beat sugar, butter and oil in large bowl until well blended. Add eggs 1 at a time, beating well after each addition. Beat in vanilla extract. Mix in dry ingredients alternately with buttermilk in 3 additions each. Mix in grated zucchini. Pour batter into prepared pan. Sprinkle chocolate chips and nuts over.

• Bake cake until tester inserted into center comes out clean, about 50 minutes. Cool cake completely in pan.

• *12 servings*

Lemon Cornmeal Cake with Raspberry Filling

Cornmeal gives this lemony cake a coarse texture that is a delightful foil for the smooth filling and whipped cream frosting. You can prepare the cake four hours ahead, making it an ideal addition to The Dessert Buffet on page 168. It would also end the Garden Party (page 92) on a light note.

FILLING

2	cups frozen unsweetened raspberries, thawed
2	tablespoons sugar
1	tablespoon cornstarch

CAKE

3/4	cup (1 1/2 sticks) unsalted butter, room temperature
3/4	cup sugar
3	large eggs
1 1/4	cups cake flour
2	teaspoons baking powder
1/4	teaspoon salt
1/2	cup yellow cornmeal
6	teaspoons grated lemon peel
2	teaspoons lemon extract

FROSTING

2	cups chilled whipping cream
2	tablespoons sugar
1	teaspoon lemon extract
3	teaspoons grated lemon peel

3/4	cup sliced almonds, toasted

• FOR FILLING: Puree berries in processor. Strain into heavy medium saucepan. Add sugar and cornstarch. Stir over medium heat until mixture boils and thickens, about 3 minutes. Cool. Cover; chill until cold, about 2 hours.

• FOR CAKE: Preheat oven to 350°F. Lightly butter 9-inch-diameter cake pan with 2-inch-high sides. Line bottom with parchment paper. Butter parchment. Dust pan with flour; shake out excess. Using electric mixer, beat butter in large bowl until fluffy. Add sugar and beat until well blended. Add eggs 1 at a time, beating well after each addition. Sift flour, baking powder and salt into medium bowl. Stir in cornmeal. Add to butter mixture and beat just until blended. Mix in lemon peel and extract.

• Transfer batter to prepared pan. Bake until cake is golden and toothpick inserted into center comes out with a few moist crumbs attached, about 35 minutes. Transfer cake to rack; cool. Using knife, cut around pan sides to loosen cake. Turn cake out. Peel off parchment.

• FOR FROSTING: Beat cream, sugar and extract in large bowl until soft peaks form. Beat in 1½ teaspoons lemon peel. Set aside ⅔ cup frosting for decoration.

• Using serrated knife, cut cake horizontally into 3 layers. Using bottom of 9-inch-diameter tart pan as aid, transfer 1 layer to platter. Spread half of filling over. Spread 1 cup frosting over filling. Top with second cake layer. Spread remaining filling over. Spread 1 cup frosting over filling. Top with third cake layer. Spread sides and top of cake with remaining frosting. Press almonds onto sides of cake. Spoon reserved ⅔ cup frosting into pastry bag fitted with medium star tip. Pipe around top edge of cake. Sprinkle top of cake with 1½ teaspoons lemon peel. *(Can be made 4 hours ahead. Cover with cake dome and refrigerate. Let cake stand at room temperature for 1 hour before serving.)*

• *12 servings*

frozen desserts

Lemon Ripple Ice Cream Pie

For the Pasta Party menu (page 34), a different kind of ice cream dessert. In this spectacular pie with its almond and graham cracker crust, the lemon curd freezes to a dense consistency, creating a refreshing contrast of textures. (You might also have this treat at the end of the South-of-the-Border Party, page 84).

LEMON CURD

- 1 cup sugar
- 6 tablespoons (3/4 stick) unsalted butter, cut into small pieces
- 1/3 cup fresh lemon juice
- 2 large eggs
- 2 large egg yolks
- 1 teaspoon grated lemon peel

CRUST

- 1 1/4 cups ground toasted almonds (about 5 ounces)
- 1 cup graham cracker crumbs (5 whole graham crackers)
- 1/4 cup plus 3 tablespoons unsalted butter, melted
- 2 teaspoons grated lemon peel
- 1/2 teaspoon almond extract

- 1/2 gallon vanilla ice cream, softened slightly
- 1 12-ounce basket strawberries, sliced, sugared to taste (optional)

- **FOR CURD:** Combine sugar, butter and lemon juice in top of double boiler. Set over pan of simmering water and stir until sugar dissolves and butter melts. Beat eggs, yolks and lemon peel in bowl until well blended. Gradually whisk warm butter mixture into egg mixture. Return mixture to double boiler and cook over simmering water until curd is thick and leaves path on back of spoon when finger is drawn across, stirring constantly, about 10 minutes; do not boil. Transfer lemon curd to bowl, whisking to smooth if necessary. Press plastic wrap directly onto surface of curd and chill until cold, at least 1 hour. *(Can be made 3 days ahead; keep refrigerated.)*

- **FOR CRUST:** Preheat oven to 325°F. Butter 9-inch-diameter springform pan with 2¾-inch-high sides. Mix almonds, graham cracker crumbs, butter, lemon peel and almond extract in medium bowl until mixture is evenly moist. Press crumbs over bottom and 1 inch up sides of prepared pan. Bake crust 8 minutes. Cool crust on rack.

- Spread half of ice cream in crust. Spoon half of lemon curd over. Spoon remaining ice cream over. Spoon remaining curd over ice cream by tablespoons. Use small knife to swirl curd into ice cream, forming pretty design. Freeze until just firm, about 1 hour. Wrap and freeze overnight. *(Can be prepared 2 days ahead; keep frozen.)* Let pie stand 10 minutes at room temperature. Cut pie into wedges and serve, spooning strawberries over if desired.

- *10 to 12 servings*

Lemon Ripple Ice Cream Pie (left);
Orange-Caramel Nut Sundaes (opposite, right);
Chocolate Brownie Sundaes (opposite, far right);

Chocolate Brownie Sundaes

Three favorites—brownies, ice cream and fudge sauce—come together in a wonderfully simple and tasty dessert. Try it at the end of the Dinner and a Movie menu (page 78) or the Pizza Party one (page 70).

1 3/4 cups all purpose flour
1 teaspoon baking powder
Pinch of salt
4 ounces unsweetened chocolate, chopped
1 cup vegetable oil
1 tablespoon instant espresso powder or instant coffee granules
2 teaspoons vanilla extract
4 large eggs
2 cups sugar

Purchased or homemade fudge sauce
2 pints ice cream

• Preheat oven to 350°F. Butter 8-inch square baking pan with 2-inch-high sides. Sift flour, baking powder and salt into small bowl. Melt chocolate in heavy small saucepan over low heat, stirring until smooth. Pour into large bowl. Add oil, espresso powder and vanilla and whisk to blend. Whisk in eggs and sugar. Stir in dry ingredients. Pour batter into prepared pan. Bake until top is dry and toothpick inserted in center comes out with moist crumbs still attached, about 30 minutes. Immediately transfer to refrigerator. Refrigerate until cold, at least 3 hours. *(Can be prepared 1 day ahead. Store in refrigerator.)*
• Heat fudge sauce if desired. Cut brownies into squares. Top with scoops of ice cream. Spoon sauce over and serve.
• *8 servings*

Orange-Caramel Nut Sundaes

A refreshing change of pace from the chocolate tart in the Dinner in the Kitchen menu (page 10).

3 oranges
1 cup firmly packed light brown sugar
10 tablespoons fresh orange juice
3 tablespoons unsalted butter

Vanilla frozen yogurt or ice cream
1/2 cup hazelnuts, toasted, husked, coarsely chopped

• Remove orange peel from oranges with vegetable peeler. Cut enough peel into very fine strips to measure 2 tablespoons. Transfer strips to heavy medium saucepan. Add sugar, juice and butter. Stir over medium heat until sugar dissolves. Increase heat and boil gently until reduced to 1 cup, about 15 minutes. Cool sauce to lukewarm. *(Can be prepared 2 days ahead. Cover sauce and oranges separately and chill. Reheat sauce to lukewarm before using.)*
• Cut white pith from oranges. Slice oranges into rounds; cut rounds into quarters. Scoop frozen yogurt into large wineglasses. Drizzle sauce over. Top with oranges and hazelnuts and serve.
• *6 servings*

mousses and puddings

Raspberry and Marsala Trifle

A purchased cake mix (spiked with Marsala for added zip) makes this elegant dessert a snap to prepare. For extra ease, you can assemble it the day before serving. It makes a lovely finale to the menu on page 132 that includes the Roast Turkey with Prosciutto, Rosemary and Garlic.

CAKE

1 18 1/2-ounce package Duncan Hines Moist Deluxe Butter Recipe Golden cake mix

2/3 cup dry Marsala

FILLING

3 12-ounce packages frozen unsweetened raspberries, thawed, drained

3 tablespoons plus 3/4 cup sugar

9 large egg yolks

1 cup dry Marsala

1 1/2 cups chilled whipping cream

1 1/2-pint basket fresh raspberries

• FOR CAKE: Butter and flour 13 x 9 x 2-inch baking pan. Prepare cake according to package instructions, substituting ⅔ cup Marsala for water. Bake cake and cool completely. Cut cake crosswise into thirds. Cut cake lengthwise into 1-inch-wide slices. Set aside.

• FOR FILLING: Mix thawed frozen raspberries and 3 tablespoons sugar in large bowl. Set aside.

• Using handheld mixer, beat egg yolks and remaining ¾ cup sugar in large metal bowl until well blended. Beat in 1 cup dry Marsala. Place bowl over saucepan of simmering water (do not let bottom of bowl touch water). Beat until mixture triples in volume and registers 160°F on thermometer, about 6 minutes. Remove bowl from over water. Cool to room temperature, whisking occasionally.

• Using electric mixer with clean dry beaters, beat ¾ cup cream in large bowl until stiff peaks form. Fold whipped cream into yolk mixture.

• Arrange enough cake slices in 12-cup trifle dish to cover bottom. Spoon 1 cup of raspberry mixture over cake, allowing some to show at sides of bowl. Pour 1½ cups filling over; smooth top. Arrange enough cake slices over filling to cover completely. Spread 1 cup raspberry mixture over, allowing some to show at sides. Pour 1½ cups filling over. Arrange enough cake slices over filling to cover completely. Spread remaining raspberry mixture over. Pour remaining filling over; smooth top. Cover and refrigerate trifle at least 4 hours or overnight.

• Using electric mixer, beat ¾ cup chilled whipping cream to stiff peaks in medium bowl. Spoon into pastry bag fitted with large star tip. Pipe whipped cream decoratively over trifle. Garnish trifle with fresh raspberries.

• *10 servings*

Raspberry and Marsala Trifle (top left); Buttermilk Bread Pudding with Creamy Chocolate Sauce (bottom left)

Buttermilk Bread Pudding with Creamy Chocolate Sauce

Quick to prepare and comforting in its simplicity, this yummy bread pudding would make a cozy conclusion to the Dinner and a Movie menu (page 78).

  3 eggs
  2 egg yolks
2/3 cup sugar
  2 cups buttermilk
2 1/2 cups half and half
  2 teaspoons vanilla extract
  9 buttermilk bread slices, crusts removed, cut into 1-inch pieces (about 6 generous cups)
    Ground nutmeg
    Creamy Chocolate Sauce (see recipe below)

• Preheat oven to 325°F. Butter 13 x 9 x 2-inch glass baking dish. Whisk eggs, yolks and sugar to blend in large bowl. Mix in buttermilk, half and half and vanilla. Add bread; let stand 5 minutes. Transfer to prepared dish. Sprinkle lightly with nutmeg. Place baking dish in large roasting pan. Add enough hot water to roasting pan to come 1 inch up sides of baking dish. Bake until pudding is firm in center but still pale in color, about 1 hour 15 minutes. Cool slightly. Serve bread pudding warm or cold, passing warm sauce separately.
• *8 servings*

Creamy Chocolate Sauce

3/4 cup whipping cream
  3 tablespoons sugar
  1 teaspoon vanilla extract
  5 ounces bittersweet (not unsweetened) or semisweet chocolate, chopped

• Combine cream, sugar and vanilla in heavy medium saucepan. Stir over medium-high heat until sugar dissolves. Reduce heat to low. Add chocolate and stir until melted. Serve warm.
• *Makes about 1 1/3 cups*

Coffee Crème Caramel

Coffee adds a welcome edge of flavor to that sweetly simple classic bistro dessert, crème caramel. Use a full-flavored regular roast coffee, such as mocha-java; do not use dark-roasted beans, as they will give the custards an unattractive appearance. Try this dessert at the end of the Bistro Supper menu (page 42).

  2 cups whipping cream
1 1/2 cups half and half
1 1/2 cups whole coffee beans, such as mocha-java (about 4 ounces)

1 1/3 cups sugar
  1/3 cup water

  3 large eggs
  5 large egg yolks
3/4 cup sugar
  2 teaspoons vanilla extract
  1/8 teaspoon salt

• Bring 2 cups whipping cream and 1½ cups half and half to boil in heavy medium saucepan. Add whole coffee beans. Remove from heat. Cover and let cream mixture steep 45 minutes. Strain through sieve; discard coffee beans.
• Combine 1⅓ cups sugar and ⅓ cup water in heavy medium saucepan. Stir over low heat until sugar dissolves. Increase heat and boil without stirring until syrup turns deep golden brown, occasionally swirling pan and brushing down sides of pan with wet pastry brush, about 10 minutes. Immediately divide caramel among eight 5- to 6-ounce custard cups. Carefully swirl cups slightly to coat bottoms and partially up sides with caramel. Set aside.
• Position rack in center of oven and preheat to 325°F. Whisk 3 large eggs, 5 large egg yolks, ¾ cup sugar, 2 teaspoons vanilla extract and ⅛ teaspoon salt in medium bowl to blend. Whisk in coffee-infused cream mixture. Ladle custard into prepared cups. Arrange cups in large baking pan. Add enough hot water to pan to come halfway up sides of cups. Bake custards until almost set,

about 50 minutes. Remove custards from water and cool. Cover and refrigerate at least 5 hours. *(Can be prepared 2 days ahead.)*
• Run small sharp knife around sides of custards to loosen. Invert onto plates.
• *8 servings*

Vanilla Flan with Raspberries

An ideal ending to the Fajita Party (see Easy Guacamole on page 102 for details).

  2 cups sugar
  1/2 cup water

  6 large eggs
  6 large egg yolks
  2 tablespoons vanilla extract
  2 cups whipping cream
2 1/2 cups milk (do not use lowfat or nonfat)
1 1/2 cups sugar

  2 cups fresh raspberries

• Preheat oven to 325°F. Combine 2 cups sugar and ½ cup water in heavy medium saucepan. Stir over low heat until sugar dissolves. Increase heat and boil without stirring until sugar caramelizes, occasionally swirling pan and brushing sides with wet pastry brush. Immediately pour caramel into two 9-inch glass pie dishes (4-cup capacity each), dividing as evenly as possible. Carefully turn dishes to coat bottom and sides with caramel.
• Whisk eggs, egg yolks and vanilla extract in large bowl to blend. Add whipping cream, milk and 1½ cups sugar and stir gently until sugar dissolves. Divide custard between caramel-lined dishes. Place in heavy large baking pan. Add enough hot water to pan to come halfway up sides of dishes. Bake until knife inserted into center of custards comes out clean, about 55 minutes. Remove custards from water and cool. Cover and refrigerate overnight. *(Can be prepared 2 days ahead.)*
• Invert custards onto platters. Sprinkle with raspberries and serve.
• *Makes two 9-inch flans*

Classic Tiramisù

This light and creamy tiramisù benefits from being refrigerated overnight, making it an ideal candidate for The Dessert Buffet on page 168. It would also work at the end of the Pasta Party (page 34).

2 (about) 4.4-ounce packages Champagne biscuits (dry 4-inch-long ladyfinger-like biscuits)
2 1/2 cups hot water
1/4 cup sugar
5 teaspoons instant espresso powder
1/4 cup brandy
2 tablespoons vanilla extract

1 7 3/4- to 8-ounce container mascarpone cheese*
3 tablespoons sifted powdered sugar
1 cup chilled whipping cream

2 tablespoons unsweetened cocoa powder
Espresso beans (optional)

• Cover bottom of 13 x 9 x 2-inch glass baking dish with single layer of biscuits. Combine water, sugar and espresso powder in large bowl and stir until sugar and espresso powder dissolve. Stir in brandy and vanilla. Pour 1 cup of espresso mixture over biscuits in baking dish. Reserve remaining espresso mixture.
• Beat mascarpone cheese and 2 tablespoons powdered sugar in medium bowl until creamy. Using electric mixer fitted with clean beaters, beat cream in another medium bowl until peaks form. Gently fold whipped cream into cheese mixture in 2 additions. Spread mixture evenly over biscuits. Dip enough biscuits into remaining espresso mixture to cover tiramisù and arrange in single layer over cheese mixture. Cover and refrigerate at least 2 hours or overnight.
• Combine cocoa powder and remaining 1 tablespoon powdered sugar in small bowl. Sift evenly over tiramisù. Garnish with espresso beans, if desired.
*Italian cream cheese available at Italian markets and some specialty foods stores. If unavailable, blend 8 ounces cream cheese with 1/4 cup whipping cream and 2 1/2 tablespoons sour cream.
• 12 servings

fruit desserts

Double-dipped Strawberries

A pretty addition to The Dessert Buffet (page 168), and a delicious nibble after drinks as a part of the Cocktails at Five menu (page 18).

36 strawberries (about two 1-pint baskets), unhulled

1 1/2 cups semisweet chocolate chips (about 9 ounces)
1 tablespoon vegetable shortening
1 1/2 cups chocolate sprinkles (about 6 ounces)

• Line large baking sheet with waxed paper. Wipe strawberries clean; pat berries dry with paper towels.
• Stir chocolate chips and shortening in top of double boiler set over simmering water until chocolate melts and mixture is smooth. Place chocolate sprinkles in shallow bowl. Holding 1 strawberry by its green top, dip 3/4 of berry into melted chocolate. Let excess chocolate drip off, then dip into chocolate sprinkles. Place on waxed-paper-lined sheet. Repeat dipping remaining strawberries into chocolate, then into sprinkles. Refrigerate until chocolate coating is firm, about 1 hour. (Can be prepared 8 hours ahead. Keep refrigerated.)
• Makes 36

Pears Poached in Red Wine

This recipe, which might stand in for the sorbet in the Bistro Supper (page 42), is a year-round delight. In summer, when peaches are in season, they can be used instead of pears.

3 cups dry red wine
1 cup sugar
1 cinnamon stick, broken into 4 pieces
1/2 vanilla bean or 2 tablespoons vanilla extract
4 whole cloves
4 firm ripe pears, peeled

Pears Poached in Red Wine

• Bring red wine, sugar, cinnamon, vanilla and whole cloves to boil in heavy large saucepan. Add pears and simmer until tender but not mushy, turning occasionally, about 15 minutes. Transfer pears and syrup to large bowl. Refrigerate until well chilled, about 4 hours. *(Can be prepared 2 days ahead.)*

• Cut pears lengthwise in half and remove cores. Starting ½ inch from stem end, make several lengthwise cuts in each pear half. Transfer pear halves to plates. Press gently on pears to fan slices. Serve pears immediately with syrup.

• *8 servings*

Peaches and Raspberries in Spiced White Wine

A fresh, fruity dessert that can be prepared ahead. Try it at the end of the Pizza Party (page **70**).

1	bottle (750 ml) Italian dry white wine, such as Pinot Bianco or Pinot Grigio
1/2	cup sugar
4	3/4 x 2-inch orange peel strips (orange part only)
3	cinnamon sticks
6	peaches
2	1/2-pint baskets raspberries Biscotti

• Combine 1 cup wine, sugar, orange peel and cinnamon in small saucepan. Stir over low heat until sugar dissolves. Increase heat; simmer 15 minutes. Remove from heat; add remaining wine.

• Blanch peaches in large pot of boiling water 20 seconds. Transfer to bowl of cold water, using slotted spoon. Drain. Pull off skin with small sharp knife. Slice peaches and transfer to large bowl. Add raspberries and wine mixture. Cover and refrigerate at least 1 hour. *(Can be prepared 6 hours ahead. Stir occasionally.)* Divide fruit and wine among glass goblets. Serve with biscotti.

• *8 servings*

Individual Pear and Maple Cobblers

If it's fall and pears are in abundance the next time you're having friends over for Dinner and a Movie (page **78**), try this old-fashioned dessert.

FILLING

3	pounds ripe Bartlett pears, peeled, quartered, cored
2/3	cup pure maple syrup
1	tablespoon plus 2 teaspoons all purpose flour
1/2	teaspoon vanilla extract
1/8	teaspoon (generous) ground nutmeg
1 1/2	tablespoons butter

TOPPING

1 1/2	cups all purpose flour
2 1/4	teaspoons baking powder
1/4	teaspoon ground nutmeg
6	tablespoons (3/4 stick) chilled unsalted butter, cut into 1/2-inch pieces
9	tablespoons half and half
9	tablespoons pure maple syrup
3/4	teaspoon vanilla extract
	Melted butter
	Sugar
	Ground nutmeg
1	cup chilled whipping cream Additional pure maple syrup

• FOR FILLING: Preheat oven to 425°F. Cut pears crosswise into ¼-inch-thick slices. Combine in large bowl with maple syrup, flour, vanilla extract and ground nutmeg. Divide among six ⅔-cup custard cups or soufflé dishes. Dot tops with butter. Bake filling until hot and bubbling, about 18 minutes.

• MEANWHILE, PREPARE TOPPING: Mix first 3 ingredients in processor. Add 6 tablespoons chilled butter and cut in until mixture resembles fine meal. Transfer to large bowl. Mix half and half, 6 tablespoons syrup and vanilla in another bowl. Add to dry ingredients; stir until just combined.

• Working quickly, drop batter in three mounds, 1 heaping tablespoon per mound, atop hot filling in each cup. Brush topping with melted butter and sprinkle with sugar and nutmeg. Immediately return cups to oven and bake 8 minutes. Reduce temperature to 375°F and bake until toppings are golden and just firm to touch, about 14 minutes. Cool at least 15 minutes.

• In medium bowl, beat 1 cup chilled cream with 3 tablespoons maple syrup to soft peaks. Serve cobblers warm with whipped cream. Drizzle additional maple syrup over.

• *6 servings*

Individual Pear and Maple Cobblers

Broiled Pink Grapefruit with Honey

This light and simple dessert might work nicely at the end of the Garden Party menu (page 92).

6   large pink grapefruit

2   tablespoons sugar
6   tablespoons honey

• Using small sharp knife, cut away all peel and white pith from 1 grapefruit. Working over large bowl, cut between membranes to release segments; add segments to bowl. Repeat with remaining grapefruit. *(Can be prepared 4 hours ahead. Cover and refrigerate.)*
• Preheat broiler. Drain grapefruit segments. Arrange segments in broiler-proof dish. Sprinkle with sugar, then drizzle honey evenly over. Place dish with grapefruit about 3 inches from heat source and broil until grapefruit begins to brown, about 4 minutes. Serve hot.
• *8 servings*

Broiled Pink Grapefruit with Honey and Ginger-Lemon Cookies

cookies

Ginger-Lemon Cookies

Offer these with the Broiled Pink Grapefruit with Honey (at left) at the end of the Garden Party (page 92).

1/2   cup (1 stick) unsalted butter, room temperature
3/4   cup plus 4 tablespoons sugar
1   large egg
1 1/4   teaspoons (packed) grated lemon peel
1/2   teaspoon vanilla extract
1   cup plus 2 tablespoons all purpose flour
1 1/2   teaspoons baking powder
1   teaspoon ground ginger
1/4   teaspoon salt

• Using electric mixer, beat butter and ¾ cup plus 1 tablespoon sugar in large bowl until smooth. Beat in egg, lemon peel and vanilla extract. Sift dry ingredients into butter mixture. Beat until blended. Cover bowl and refrigerate dough until well chilled, about 1 hour.
• Preheat oven to 325°F. Line 2 heavy large baking sheets with parchment paper. Using floured hands, roll heaping teaspoonfuls of chilled dough into balls. Arrange on sheets, spacing 2 inches apart. Place remaining 3 tablespoons sugar into small bowl. Moisten bottom of measuring cup with water. Dip bottom of cup into sugar. Press cup onto 1 dough ball, flattening to ⅓-inch thickness. Repeat flattening with remaining dough, dipping cup into sugar before flattening each dough ball.
• Bake cookies until golden brown, about 18 minutes. Transfer cookies to rack and cool completely. *(Cookies can be prepared 1 day ahead. Store in airtight container at room temperature.)*
• *Makes about 45*

Pine Nut-Almond Macaroons

These cookies are an easy, do-ahead dessert, and could be added to the Lunch on the Terrace menu (page 28), or offered instead of the *pots de crème.* (There will be plenty left over for snacking.)

1/4   cup Marsala
3   tablespoons dried currants

3/4   cup toasted slivered almonds
1/2   cup toasted pine nuts
2/3   cup sugar
1   tablespoon all purpose flour
1   large egg white
1/8   teaspoon (generous) almond extract
1   cup pine nuts (about 4½ ounces)

• Preheat oven to 350°F. Line large cookie sheet with foil. Combine Marsala and currants in heavy small saucepan. Cook over medium heat until liquid evaporates, about 5 minutes. Cool.
• Finely grind almonds and ½ cup toasted pine nuts with sugar and flour in processor. Mix egg white with extract in medium bowl. Add to processor and blend until dough forms ball. Place dough in bowl. Mix in currants. Shape dough between palms into ¾-inch-diameter balls. Roll in 1 cup pine nuts to cover, pressing to adhere. Flatten each to 1½-inch round. Space evenly on cookie sheet. Bake until golden brown, about 15 minutes. Cool slightly. Remove cookies from foil using metal spatula and cool on rack. *(Can be prepared 4 days ahead. Store cookies in airtight container at room temperature.)*
• *Makes about 22*

Macadamia Nut-Chocolate Chip Refrigerator Cookies

These are the homemade version of the rolls of cookie dough you can buy at the supermarket, made special by the addition of pecans and macadamia nuts. You can keep the dough in the refrigerator up to three days; then slice and bake whenever the urge for a cookie hits. Pack some up for the Picnic in the Country (page 48).

3/4 cup (1 1/2 sticks) unsalted butter, room temperature
3/4 cup (packed) golden brown sugar
2/3 cup powdered sugar
1 large egg
1 teaspoon vanilla extract
2 1/2 cups all purpose flour
1 teaspoon baking soda
1 teaspoon salt
2 cups semisweet chocolate chips (about 12 ounces)
1 cup chopped macadamia nuts (about 4 1/2 ounces)
1/3 cup chopped pecans (about 1 ounce)

• Using electric mixer, beat butter, brown sugar and powdered sugar in large bowl until fluffy. Beat in egg and vanilla. Sift flour, baking soda and salt into medium bowl. Add to butter mixture and beat until blended. Stir in chocolate chips, macadamia nuts and pecans. Place 2 sheets plastic wrap on work surface. Spoon dough in 12-inch-long strip down center of each plastic sheet, dividing equally. Form each dough strip into 12-inch-long log. Wrap in plastic and refrigerate 1 hour. *(Can be prepared 3 days ahead. Keep refrigerated.)*
• Preheat oven to 325°F. Using sharp knife, cut dough into 1/2-inch-thick slices. Arrange slices on large baking sheets. Bake until cookies are light golden brown, about 14 minutes. Transfer sheets to racks and cool 5 minutes. Transfer cookies to racks and cool.
• *Makes about 40*

Fudge-filled Butter Cookies

Yummy sandwich cookies that would be a hit with all the kids at the Family Reunion (page 64).

COOKIES
1 cup (2 sticks) unsalted butter, room temperature
3/4 cup powdered sugar
2 cups unbleached all purpose flour
1/2 teaspoon almond extract
Pinch of salt

FILLING
4 ounces semisweet chocolate
2 1/2 tablespoons unsalted butter
2 1/2 tablespoons whipping cream
1/2 cup powdered sugar
1/4 teaspoon almond extract

• FOR COOKIES: Preheat oven to 350°F. Beat butter and sugar in large bowl until creamy. Mix in flour, extract and salt, stirring until dough holds together. Form dough by rounded teaspoonfuls into balls. Place balls on ungreased large baking sheets, spacing 2 inches apart. Flatten slightly with bottom of glass.
• Bake cookies until light brown, about 14 minutes. Transfer sheets to racks and cool 5 minutes. Transfer cookies to racks and cool completely.
• FOR FILLING: Finely chop chocolate in processor. Combine butter and cream in small saucepan. Bring to boil. With processor running, gradually add butter mixture to chocolate and process until smooth. Transfer to medium bowl. Add sugar and almond extract and stir until mixture is smooth. Cool filling until spreadable, about 5 minutes.
• Spread about 1 teaspoon filling on flat side of half of cookies. Top with remaining cookies, flat side down, creating sandwiches. *(Can be prepared 2 days ahead. Store sandwiches in airtight container at room temperature.)*
• *Makes about 3 dozen*

Cinnamon-Raisin Biscotti

These crisp, low-fat cookies are just right for dipping into dessert wine or cappuccino. Set up a coffee bar at The Dessert Buffet (page 168) and place them there, or have them after Dinner in the Kitchen (page 10).

1 large egg
1/2 cup sugar
1 tablespoon brandy
1 teaspoon vanilla extract
3/4 cup plus 2 tablespoons all purpose flour
3/4 teaspoon baking powder
3/4 teaspoon ground cinnamon
1/4 teaspoon (generous) salt
1/3 cup raisins
1/3 cup whole almonds, toasted

• Preheat oven to 375°F. Lightly grease heavy large baking sheet. Using handheld electric mixer, beat egg and sugar in medium bowl until very thick and fluffy, about 2 minutes. Beat in brandy and vanilla. Sift flour, baking powder, cinnamon and salt into egg mixture and blend well. Mix in raisins and almonds. Spoon dough onto prepared sheet to form 10- to 11-inch strip. Using moistened fingertips, shape dough into neat 11-inch-long by 2 1/2-inch-wide log.
• Bake until log just begins to brown and feels firm to touch, about 20 minutes. Cool cookie log on sheet 15 minutes. Maintain oven temperature.
• Transfer cookie log to work surface. Using serrated knife, cut crosswise into 1/3 inch wide slices. Arrange slices on same baking sheet. Bake 10 minutes. Turn slices over. Bake until beginning to color, about 8 minutes longer. Cool cookies completely on baking sheet (cookies will become very crisp). *(Can be prepared 1 week ahead. Store in airtight container at room temperature.)*
• *Makes about 2 dozen*

the
dessert
buffet

- Lemon Cornmeal Cake with Raspberry Filling (page 159)

- Milk Chocolate-Pecan Tartlets (page 155)

Party for Twelve — Classic Tiramisù (page 164)

- Cinnamon-Raisin Biscotti (page 167)

- Double-dipped Strawberries (page 164)

- Champagne, Coffee and Liqueurs

When you'd like to bring a little elegance to the party, and there isn't the time (or energy) for a carefully planned sit-down dinner, the dessert buffet can be the ideal "meal." Add Champagne, coffee and liqueurs to a lavish selection of (made-ahead) sweets, and you have a sophisticated spread that can be readied in minutes. ★ Like the typical English "department store" tea, the dessert buffet can work in the late afternoon, at a wedding or baby shower. It can also be a lovely ending to an evening out, allowing the cook the freedom to attend the event and still return home right afterward to host a picture-perfect, late-night party. And it is easily made smaller or larger simply by subtracting or adding desserts. ★ When every dish is sweet, the need for nuances of taste and texture challenges the composition of the menu.

The invitation to each guest to try several desserts should be backed up by the distinctions among them. This menu illustrates a tempting spectrum, from the creamiest tiramisù and a fruit-filled crumbly layer cake to crisp, raisin-almond *biscotti* and densely chocolate tartlets. Strawberries, dipped in melted chocolate and then sprinkles, decorate and delight. The whole spread will indulge 12 to 15 people; to serve another 5 or so, add a dessert that serves at least 6. But make it something altogether different, possibly a beautiful fruit pie.

index

Page numbers in *italics* indicate color photographs.

THE PERSONALIZED PARTY:
CREATING A MENU
OF YOUR OWN DESIGN

In an effort to make this book as flexible and as useful as possible, we've stressed the mix-and-match aspect of menu planning throughout. In the back half of the book, every recipe begins with a note that guides you to a menu in the front of the book where the recipe will work. Likewise, this list takes the recipes in the front of the book and leads you to those in the back that will substitute beautifully. Creating a menu that suits you, your guests, the season, whatever, has never been easier.

Index

Index

Index

176
Index
Index

acknowledgments

The following people contributed the
recipes included in this book:
Mary Barber; Bar Italia, St. Louis, Missouri;
Melanie Barnard; Joe Bartolotta; Patrick
Bermingham; Pam Blanton; Carole Bloom;
Sidney and Jim Bonnet; Anne Boulard;
Blair Box; Blythe Boyd; Jean and Walt
Boylan; Jill Branch; Susan Burnside; By
Word of Mouth, Fort Lauderdale, Florida;
Stacy L. Callahan; Jonna and John Carls;
Richard Chamberlain; Sara Corpening;
Patti and David Cottle; Russell Cronkhite;
Amy Willard Cross; Lane Crowther; Tony
DiSalvo; Brooke Dojny; Roberto Donna;
Donna's, Baltimore, Maryland; Jonathan
Eismann; Crystal Ettridge; Karen Fisher;
Brad Fox; Judy Hasselkus; Wendy Hutzler;
Jim Jensvold; Karen Kaplan; Kathleen's
Kuisine, Arnold, Maryland; Jeanne Thiel
Kelley; Susan and Larry Kessler; Kristine
Kidd; Elinor Klivans; David and Dey Young
Ladd; Lantana's, Grand Cayman, British
West Indies; Ellen Lebow; Jessica Leighton;
Sarabeth Levine; Michael McLaughlin;
Selma Brown Morrow; John Muse;
Bradley Ogden; Leslie Patson; Presidio
Grill, Tucson, Arizona; Tammy
Randerman; Betty Rosbottom; Richard
Sax; Carolyn Schmitz; Marie Simmons;
Joan and Richard Skelton; Jessica L. Smith;
Richard Snyder; Scott Snyder; Ilana
Sharlin Stone; Geetha Subramanian;
Steve Sunyog; Tapawingo, Ellsworth,
Michigan; Kevin Taylor; Sarah Tenaglia;
Suzie and Joe Tierney; Brad and Susie
Tjossem; Wayne Turett; Dave Tyson;
Unicorn Village Restaurant, North
Miami, Florida; Lorraine Vassalo; Vinci,
Chicago, Illinois; The Watercress Cafe,
Lake Buena Vista, Florida.

The following people contributed the
photographs included in this book:
Jack Andersen; David Bishop; Cynthia
Brown; Angie Norwood Browne;
Burke/Triolo Studios; Wyatt Counts;
Deborah Denker; Julie Dennis; Michael
Deuson; Fernando Diez; Alison Duke;
Phillip Esparza; Deborah Feingold; Mark
Ferri; John Reed Forsman; Beth Galton;
Paul Gersten; Henry Hamamoto; Jim
Hansen; Charles Imstepf; Kathryn
Kleinman; Mark Laita; Laurie Lambrecht;
Lannen/Kelly; Brian Leatart; Bret Lopez;
Andrew Martin; Judd Pilossof; Aaron
Rapoport; Steven Rothfeld; Andrew Sacks;
Jeff Sarpa; Ellen Silverman; Mark Thomas;
Elizabeth Zeschin.

The original photography for this book,
which appears on the jacket and pages 2,
5, 6, 10, 18, 19, 28, 34, 42, 48, 49, 56, 64,
70, 78, 84, 92 and 168 was done by Ric
Cohn. Prop Stylist: Francine Matalon
Degni. Food Stylist: Delores Custer. Food
Stylist: Marie Haycox.

Accessories for original photography:
Jacket and page 18: ANNIEGLASS, (800)
347-6133; LCR, Westport, CT; Puiforcat,
(800) 993-2580; Sasaki, New York, NY;
Lalique, (800) 993-2580; Gino Cenedes
Figlio; E&M Glass; Christofle; Warwick
Glassblowing of Greenwich, CT; Alessi;
BARNEYS NEW YORK. On page 28:
Rooms & Gardens, New York, NY; Bill
Goldsmith designs for Site Corot., (212)
686-0808; Lexington Gardens, New York,
NY. On page 42: Williams-Sonoma, (800)
541-2233; Schott Zweisel Corp., Yonkers,
NY On page 48: Twin Fires, New York, NY;
Palecek, Richmond, CA; Craft Caravan,
New York, NY; PGH Antiques, New York,
NY; Ad Hoc Softwares, New York, NY. On
page 56: PGH Antiques. On page 64:
Kate's Paperie, New York, NY. On page 78:
PGH Antiques; Twin Fires; ANNIEGLASS.
On page 92: Paleck. On page 168: Barton-
Sharpe, New York, NY; Tudor Rose
Antiques, New York, NY; BARNEYS
NEW YORK.